AMERICAN KNIVES

FIGURE
1

Francis E. Brownell as a private in the 11th New York Regiment or Ellsworth's Zouaves in 1861. Note the bowie knife thrust through his belt. When the regiment marched into Alexandria, Va., Ellsworth was killed by a civilian who was in turn shot by Brownell. For this, Brownell received the Congressional Medal of Honor and the dagger illustrated in figure 86. NATIONAL ARCHIVES

AMERICAN KNIVES

THE FIRST HISTORY
AND
COLLECTORS' GUIDE

by
Harold L. Peterson

THE GUN ROOM PRESS

PRINTED IN THE UNITED STATES OF AMERICA
Library of Congress Catalog Card Number 58-7523

Reprint Edition 1993

Published By
    The Gun Room Press
    Highland Park, NJ 08904

By Arrangement With Copyright Owner
    Mrs. Harold Peterson

ISBN 0-88227-016-8

TO MY CHILDREN

Harold Jr., and Kristin Dorothy,
who believe every home
should have an armory

During the last ten years knife collecting has suddenly become a popular hobby. Where once only a few connoisseurs displayed interest, a large group of enthusiasts now avidly seek both the knives themselves and knowledge about them.

Because the field is so new, there is no place for most of these neophytes to turn for ready information. Unlike most other areas of collecting, no vast list of references on the subject can be found at the public library. Knowledge, like the field itself, is in its infancy. A general guide has been needed to set forth the broad framework of the subject and lay the groundwork for future more-detailed studies as a continuing and more highly specialized interest warrants their publication.

It is with this need in mind that the present work has been undertaken. It represents some twenty-five years of interest and collecting. Since a man must walk before he can run, this is designed as a primer or basic reader. As such it will delineate the subject and establish a foundation on which later works can be built. Almost every one of the chapter headings in this work merits a book of its own, and it is hoped that these can eventually be produced when the climate of interest has reached a sufficient level to make them practical and desirable. Meanwhile perhaps this volume can serve as an entering wedge and a point of departure.

In the preparation of this book I have had the wholehearted and enthusiastic support of a number of very generous people. Without their help, it could not have been done. It would be impossible to name all who have aided and assisted me, but it would be equally impossible to overlook special thanks to the following:

To Robert L. Miller and Bluford W. Muir, who once again have helped tremendously with the illustrations.

To Leonard A. Heinrich of the Metropolitan Museum of Art, George Keester of the U. S. Naval Academy Museum, Col. Frederick P. Todd and Milton F. Perry of the West Point Museum, C. Malcolm Watkins, Robert A. Elder, Mendel Peterson, Edgar M. Howell and Craddock Goins of the U. S. National Museum, G. B. Colling of the War Memorial Museum of Virginia, Richard Koke and Bella C. Landauer of the New-York Historical Society, Edwin H. Carpenter, Jr., of the New York Public Library, Dolores Cadell of the San Francisco Public Library, Dr. Heribert Seitz of the Kungliga

PREFACE

Armé Museum, Stockholm, Claude Blair of the Victoria and Albert Museum, London, and W. D. Thorburn of the Scottish United Services Museum, Edinburgh, who placed their own knowledge and all the resources of their institutions at my disposal.

To Robert Abels, William A. Allbaugh, III, Joe W. Bates, John S. du Mont, Herb Glass, Leon C. Jackson, Col. B. R. Lewis, Ben Palmer, Leonard D. Pelton, William Shermerluk and William O. Sweet, advanced collectors all, who lent me specimens for study, allowed me the use of their own research notes and in some instances read portions of the manuscript.

To W. F. Moran, Jr., and W. D. Randall, Jr., manufacturers of fine modern knives, who freely discussed the theories and techniques of knifemaking, provided data on processes and checked my discussions of the subject for accuracy.

To Lt. Col. Robert Calland of the U. S. Marine Corps Infantry Equipment Board, Dr. Harry Thompson of the Office of the Chief of Ordnance, U. S. Army, and Lewis D. Bement of the American Cutlery Manufacturers Association for valuable advice and data from their own experience and the records under their supervision.

Finally, to my wife, Dorothy, who has patiently borne with "one more book."

Harold L. Peterson

Arlington, Virginia
1957

CONTENTS

CHAPTER I

KNIFE NAMES

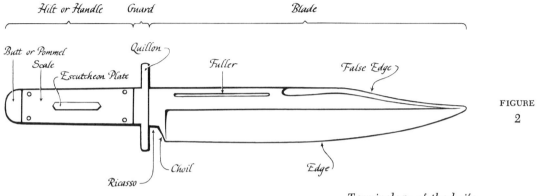

FIGURE

2

Terminology of the knife.

WHEN collectors begin to talk about their favorite topic they are apt to use a language that is often incomprehensible to the average layman. No matter whether they discuss paperweights, Chinese porcelain or ancient weapons, they soon find themselves using a vocabulary of technical terms which are seldom heard by the man in the street. They do not talk this way solely to confuse their wives or impress their uninitiated listeners, though this has often been asserted. Rather these words convey to them the precise structure, color, condition, age or type of piece more clearly and quickly than a long description made up of more general, and necessarily vaguer, words. It is far easier, for instance, to say "choil" than "the angle at the end of the edge of the blade nearest the hilt where it turns up to form a narrower squared section just in front of the handle."

This, then, is the function of technical terms: they provide a quick accurate means of communication between collectors. To perform this function, these terms must be clearly and rigidly defined and both parties must understand the definitions. Some of the terms relating to knives have been used loosely by a number of writers, and there is a difference in usage between American and English cutlers. Because of the natural confusion caused by such differences it is necessary here at the very beginning to indicate clearly the precise meanings of the technical terms and phrases as they are used in the following chapters.

First, however, there are a few words in everyday usage that need a little technical treatment because of their very general nature. These are the words "dagger," "knife" and "dirk." There has been a tendency to use these words almost synonymously, especially in the popular press, and they do have many points in common. But at the same time there are also differences in connotation. In pure usage, the dagger, always a weapon, should have a symmetrical tapering blade with two, three or even four edges and a sharp point. It is primarily designed for thrusting or stabbing. The knife, sometimes a weapon, sometimes a tool, should have a single edge for each blade, though the back can be sharpened for a short distance near the point. It is designed primarily for cutting but can also be used for thrusting. The dirk is a variant of the knife. In its original form it was a weapon with an evenly tapered blade sharpened on one edge. In the late eighteenth and early nineteenth centuries, however, the name was applied to all the short side arms carried by naval officers. Thus it included true daggers and sharply curved knives almost of cutlass length.

All knives are described in a horizontal position with the edge down, the hilt or handle to the viewer's left and the point to his right. When the knife is in this position, the side toward the viewer is the obverse. The side away from him is the reverse. A relative position toward the point is forward, toward the hilt is backward. With a folding knife, the position is determined by placing the largest or principal blade to the viewer's right, again edge down. Since true daggers are symmetrical, it is often impossible to determine obverse from reverse except through secondary structures, and then it is seldom done.

FIGURE
3

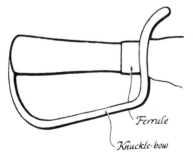

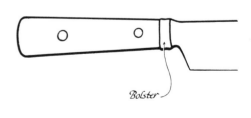

Ferrule

Knuckle-bow

Bolster

The principal part of any knife is the blade, and several technical terms are used to describe it. First there is the sharpened side, which is known as the edge. The opposite side is the back. Sometimes the back is sharpened for a short distance near the point, and this is called the false edge. If the back is beveled but not sharpened, it is called a swage. Once in a great while a groove, known as a fuller, is cut into the blade. A pocketknife almost always has a short groove, but in such blades it is known as a nail mark or nail nick. Near the hilt there is frequently a squared section of the blade without an edge which is called a ricasso. When a knife does not have a guard there is frequently a molding between the base of the blade and the grips. Sometimes it is forged integrally with the blade, and sometimes it is made separately and slipped into place when the knife is assembled. Either way it is known as a bolster. On knives with bolsters or with narrow ricassos, the portion of the blade between the bolster or the narrow section and the edge is known as the choil. Normally this is at almost a right angle to the edge, and on knives without guards it helps prevent the fingers from slipping forward along the edge. The narrow portion of the blade which passes through the handle and is riveted in place is called the tang.

Blade edges may be ground in four principal manners. These are named from their appearance when viewed in cross section: the "V" grind, the cannel or rolled edge, the hollow grind, and the concave grind. These can best be understood by referring to the accompanying diagram.

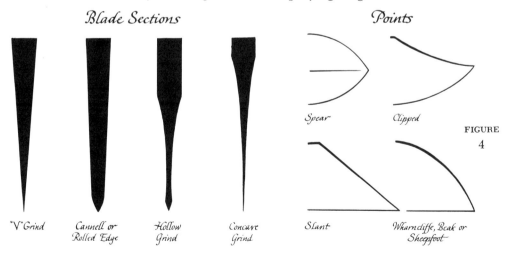

Blade Sections   *Points*

Spear   *Clipped*

FIGURE 4

"V" Grind   Cannell or Rolled Edge   Hollow Grind   Concave Grind   Slant   Wharncliffe, Beak or Sheepfoot

Blade sections and points.

As a final comment on blades, there are three principal types of points. When back and edge come together in symmetrical convex arcs, it is called a spear point. When the back swoops to meet the edge in a concave arc, it is called a clipped point. And when the back suddenly angles toward the edge in a straight line, it is called a slanted point. In pocketknives there is often a fourth point with the edge straight and the back sweeping to meet it in a convex arc. This is called a beak point or Wharncliffe point for the sixteenth-century Earl of Wharncliffe who is supposed to have developed it. (Actually it had been in use since Roman times.)

FIGURE
5

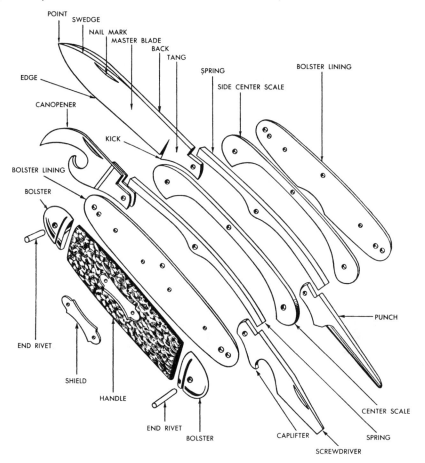

The parts of a pocketknife. REPRODUCED FROM The Cutlery Story by LEWIS D. BEMENT. COURTESY OF ASSOCIATED CUTLERY INDUSTRIES.

Knife handles, or hilts, come in a great variety of patterns, and thus there are many terms relating to them. The part seized by the hand is called the grips. If this is composed of two pieces, one fastened on each side of the tang, the individual pieces are known as scales. The end of the hilt farthest from the blade is known as the pommel or the butt.

To complicate matters somewhat, these terms are altered in meaning when applied to pocketknives. Then the word scales is used for the metal linings of the slots into which the blades fold, and the outer covering which is held by the hand is just called the covering or the handle. On pocketknives also, the term "bolster" is applied to the metal caps at each end of the handle and not to any structure of the blade.

Some hunting knives and almost all fighting knives and daggers have guards to protect the hand. Sometimes these consist of a simple plate between the grips and the blade. If the plate is relatively large, it is frequently dignified with the name counter-guard. If the guard consists of a crossbar, the two arms are called the quillons; and if there is a branch joining the guard and pommel to offer full protection for the hand, it is known as a knuckle-bow.

These are the principal technical terms used to describe knives. At first glance it may seem a forbidding list. Actually there are only twenty-five of them, and most are shown in the accompanying diagrams for ease in visualization. Once they are mastered it is amazing to notice how much simpler and easier it is to describe a given specimen—and how greatly the other members of the family are impressed!

KNIVES OF THE EXPLORERS AND COLONISTS

FIGURE
6

Scramasax of the late 8th century with its original hilt.

THE METROPOLITAN MUSEUM OF ART

SOME 960 years ago the hardy sea rovers of Leif Ericson and Biarni Heriulfson landed on the rugged and inhospitable shores of America. With them came the first European metal knives. Thrust through the belts of these rough bearded warriors were the famous Viking scramasaxes, weapons so highly prized, it is said, that they never left their owner's side day or night.

As each succeeding group of explorers or colonists arrived they brought their knives and daggers with them. To each they were his most personal and indispensable weapon. In 1541 Hernando de Soto, surprised by the Indians in a night attack at Chicaça, rushed from the flaming building where he had been sleeping to rally the defense. He had no time to buckle on his sword, but his dagger was in his belt as he mounted his horse and seized a lance. A century later in the English colonies the situation was the same, and so throughout the entire colonial period. Everyone had a knife. It was unthinkable that anyone should not. As long as a man was required to defend his life, to obtain or produce his own food or to fashion articles from raw materials, a knife was a constant necessity. It has been only during the last half century when an age of specialization has begun to provide ready-made goods to satisfy every desire that the average man has found it possible to lay his knife aside for considerable periods of time.

A study of the knives used in America during the early years shows a gradual evolution of types that set the stage for the nineteenth century, the greatest period of knife manufacture and use in American history. Through the examination of early documents and surviving specimens, aided by a knowledge of contemporary European practices, it is possible to obtain quite a clear understanding of this evolution and a good impression of just what the treasured knives of these explorers and colonists looked like and how they were used.

First came the scramasaxes, of which the Vikings were so fond. These massive weapons boasted the largest blades to be used in America before the advent of the bowie knife some 830 years later. Ranging in length up to twenty inches, they were single-edged and usually had a slanted point. The finer specimens were often inlaid with runic inscriptions or geometric designs. Although they were all-purpose knives, equally useful for cutting meat or self-defense, there was normally no guard. They were worn in a scabbard at the belt at all times, even after death when they were usually buried with their owner. The scramasax was in reality a little sword and it was used like one for both cutting and thrusting.

After the brief visits of the Vikings, there was an interval of over five hundred years when no European knives reached America. Then, shortly after 1500, the Spanish influx began in the South and Southwest. The records of these early Spanish expeditions take daggers for granted and so do not provide details on the exact types used. Several kinds were popular in Spain at the time, however, and it is logical to assume that they were also used here. There were the eared dagger, the rondel dagger and some early versions of the quillon dagger.

The eared dagger took its name from two discs which flared out from either side of the pommel. In the early specimens these discs were almost parallel. As time passed, they began to flare out more and more until, after 1550, they formed almost a straight line perpendicular to the grips. The grips themselves were formed from the exceptionally thick tang of the blade covered on either side with thin plaques of bone, ivory, horn, metal or wood, which were continued to cover the outside of the pommel discs also. In the finer specimens these plaques were usually engraved or inlaid with Moorish or Near-Eastern traceries picked out in colors. There was no guard, but a spool-shaped cylinder of metal was inserted between the grips and the blade. This and the edges of the tang were often damascened in gold.

During the early 1500's the blades of the eared daggers were normally double-edged. There was a pronounced ricasso next to the hilt, usually longer on one edge than the other. Contrasting with the fine decorative work, the blade itself was apt to be ground irregularly.

The eared dagger was worn in a sheath of wood covered with leather. Sometimes it was attached to the right side of the belt, sometimes thrust through it. At other times it was fastened to the back of a purse which in turn was worn on the right of the belt.

The design of the eared dagger originated at the eastern end of the Mediterranean. From there it passed into Italy and Spain through commerce and the Moorish conquests. It was never so popular in northern and western Europe. The eared daggers were perhaps the finest and most expensive daggers of their era, much prized by the fashionable nobility, a number of whom accompanied most of the Spanish expeditions.

The second form of dagger, the rondel, was more widely used. It developed about the middle of the fourteenth century and persisted well past the middle of the sixteenth throughout all the countries of western Europe. Because of its simplicity it was also more apt to be carried by the lower officers and common soldiers, although finely made and highly decorated specimens are also known.

The name of the dagger is taken from the two flat discs or rondels which formed the pommel and guard. Between these the grips usually consisted of a simple cylinder bored out for the tang to pass through. Sometimes, however, two-piece grips or scales riveted through the tang were used. The rondels were usually metal or wood or bone covered on both sides with plates of metal. The grips were normally wood, though horn, bone or metal was occasionally substituted.

The blades of the rondel daggers were made in a greater variety than the eared daggers. During the sixteenth century they were normally long and thin, frequently diamond-shaped in cross section. Sometimes, however, they were double-edged or even single-edged with a flat back. In these instances the blade was often thickened near the point, changing to a sturdy diamond section. The weapon's main function was the thrust, and for that a strong point was needed.

The rondel dagger was also worn in a greater variety of ways than the eared dagger. It was enclosed in a scabbard of wood covered with leather, and often there was a long metal tip. Contemporary paintings show the

FIGURE
7

Scramasax blade of the 11th century with typical slanted point.

STATENS HISTORISKA MUSEET, STOCKHOLM

FIGURE
8

Fine Italian eared dagger, 1530–1560.   THE METROPOLITAN MUSEUM OF ART

FIGURE
9

Simple Spanish eared dagger with hilt and blade forged from one piece of steel, 16th century.   THE METROPOLITAN MUSEUM OF ART

FIGURE
10

French rondel dagger, about 1450. The pommel and guard are built up of successive layers of bone, brass, bone and iron. The sides of the grips are covered with bone and brass.   THE METROPOLITAN MUSEUM OF ART

FIGURE
11

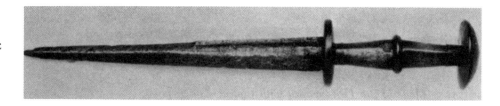

French rondel dagger of the late 15th century. The pommel and guard are brass; the grips are wood with a brass ring around the center.

THE METROPOLITAN MUSEUM OF ART

dagger attached to the sword belt or thrust through it, sometimes on the right side, sometimes in the back with the hilt to the right, and sometimes perpendicularly directly in front. Often there are thongs that seem to be attached to the sheath and looped around the belt so that the position of the dagger could be shifted at will. Like the eared dagger, the rondel was also sometimes attached to a purse.

The third type of dagger was known as the quillon or sword-hilted dagger. This interesting weapon received its name because it possessed a cross-guard or quillons and so resembled a miniature sword. It was made in a greater variety of patterns and was more widely used than either of its associates. The quillons at this period were normally small and served no real defensive purpose. Their principal function undoubtedly was to prevent the hand from slipping forward over the blade during a thrust. The pommels were metal and might have any of a number of shapes: mushroom, spherical, melon or fishtail, to name a few of the commoner ones. The grips were almost always made of one piece of wood, sometimes carved to afford a better hold. The blades most often resembled those of the rondel daggers, but there was variation among them, too—double-edged, single-edged, straight or curved. Like the rondel dagger, the quillon dagger was worn in a number of ways but most often either on the right side or at the back.

All three of the daggers thus far described were primarily weapons of offense. They were tools designed for thrusting or stabbing, with no provision for parrying an opponent's attack. The soldier of the early 1500's was not a skilled knife-fighter in the modern sense. The scientific techniques and the theories of feints and carefully co-ordinated footwork were unknown to him. He relied on his armor for protection and was primarily interested in

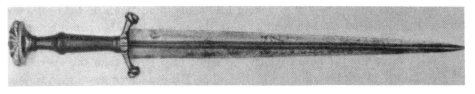

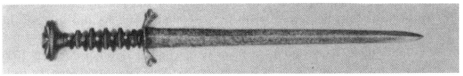

FIGURE
12

Early 16th-century quillon daggers with mushroom pommels. The upper dagger has modern grips. AUTHOR'S COLLECTION

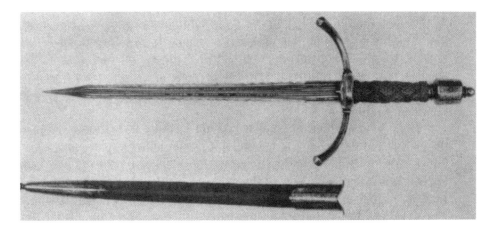

FIGURE
13

Fine quillon dagger of about 1660. The pommel and guard are damascened in gold, and the sheath is covered with green velvet. NATIONAL PARK SERVICE

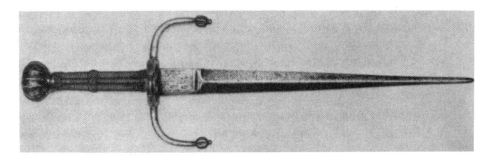

FIGURE
14

A simple quillon dagger such as a common soldier might have worn, second half of the 16th century. AUTHOR'S COLLECTION

his dagger as a means of attacking his enemy. Sometimes he held his knife in the approved modern manner with the blade above his hand, but more often he held it blade downward. He was more interested in obtaining the extra force for his blows which the latter grip gave, than the speed and versatility of strokes afforded by the other. His opponent was a man trained like himself, standing solidly and not a shifting and rapidly moving target. Hitting the opponent was relatively easy, but when he did hit, he also had to penetrate.

A radical change in these theories of combat developed about 1535. With it came an alteration in dagger design. This innovation was the technique of fighting with sword and dagger at the same time. In such combat, a rapier was held in the right hand and a dagger in the left. The attack was made primarily with the sword, the defense with the dagger, but both weapons also served the alternate function when opportunity or need arose. At the same time the techniques of knife-fighting also underwent modification. There were still no definite parries or guards, but George Silver, the famous English swordsman, described the theory of continual motion coupled with swift thrusts at exposed portions of an opponent's body as soon as they came within reach. This was the beginning of the modern school of fighting.

These new methods of combat brought changes in both the design of the dagger and the manner of holding it. In order either to parry an enemy's rapier thrust or to have the speed and dexterity necessary for the new knife attacks, it was necessary to hold the dagger with the blade above the hand. In order to protect the hand and also to hold an opponent's blade, the quillons were lengthened and frequently curved forward along the blade. Usually a ring or *anneau* was added to one side of the quillons as further protection for the knuckles. All mountings were made of iron and the wooden grips were usually bound with wire. The blades needed to be strong, yet light, and thus they were often deeply grooved and pierced. Usually they were double-edged, and sometimes the point was reinforced. These new daggers were called poignards or left-hand daggers.

The left-hand dagger is of especial interest to American collectors. It is the first type of which there is definite and specific evidence concerning its presence here. In 1564 French Huguenots founded a colony which they named Fort Caroline near present-day Jacksonville, Florida. With them was an artist, Jacques Le Moyne, who painted many pictures of events in the colony. The Spanish massacred the French settlers in 1565, but Le Moyne's pictures survived and were later engraved and printed. In them he clearly shows the left-hand dagger worn perpendicularly in front of the right hip and horizontally across the back. Some thirty-seven years later, a Spaniard, Don Luís de Velasco, who accompanied an expedition into New Mexico, mentioned that he was taking with him "a sword and a gilded dagger with their waist belts stitched with purple, yellow and white silk." At this period, a sword and dagger combination would undoubtedly have consisted of a rapier and a left-hand dagger.

With the coming of the seventeenth century a specialized form of the left-hand dagger developed in Spain and Italy. This is known to collectors today as the *main gauche,* which actually means "left hand" in French. In addition to the long quillons it had a wide triangular knuckle-bow as an extra protection. The blade also was frequently single-edged and sometimes equipped with a series of teeth near the hilt designed to catch an enemy's sword.

Details from Le Moyne's pictures of the French in Florida, 1564, showing two methods of wearing the quillon dagger.   FIGURE
15

R. Holata Outina .

In 1607 the first permanent English settlement in America was begun at Jamestown. With it the emphasis on weapons began to shift from southern Europe to England and the Low Countries. The English used some of the same kinds of daggers as the Spanish, but mostly they carried knives which were typically their own.

The earliest of these was the kidney dagger. A simply designed all-purpose knife, it had been used throughout northern Europe since about 1350. It owed its name to two globular swellings at the base of the grips which served in place of a guard to prevent the hand from sliding onto the blade. The grips, including these lobes, were usually carved from one piece of wood, ivy root being most popular. But sometimes horn or even bone hilts are encountered. Usually there was a thin plate of iron, brass or lead between the hilt and the blade, and often there was a metal washer under the tang rivet at the pommel. Most of the blades were single-edged. Some were double-edged, however, and sometimes the points were reinforced. They were worn in a scabbard attached by thongs to the belt either perpendicularly in front or at the right side. Because of their simplicity and all-round usefulness, kidney daggers were very popular with the poorer classes. Finely made specimens, on the other hand, were also used by the wealthy until shortly after 1650, when the type began to disappear.

When it came to the quillon daggers, the English also developed a form that was strictly their own. There was no separate pommel, simply a butt. The grips were carved from a single piece of wood, again probably ivy root, or horn. The short quillons, if decorated at all, were usually inlaid with silver. The blades might be curved or straight, single-edged, double-edged, reinforced at the point, or heavy diamond-shaped the entire length. There was always a definite ricasso, usually etched. The blades are also frequently dated. They were carried in sheaths in much the same manner as the kidney daggers, and frequently there were places for one or two smaller knives in the same scabbard.

These were the most popular knives in England from 1600 to 1650, and it is probable that they were the most popular ones in the English colonies here also. There is, however, no specific evidence. The early records contain many references to daggers and knives. There were also famous incidents such as the one in which little Miles Standish killed a huge Indian with a knife in a locked room at Wessagusset while three of his followers took care of a similar number of other warriors. In no instance, however,

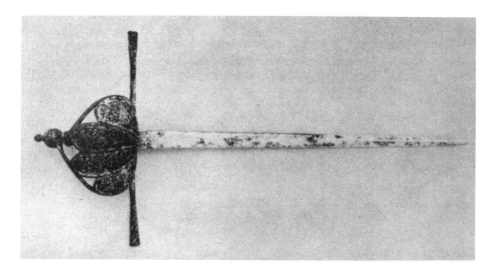

Spanish main gauche, *about 1600.*   THE METROPOLITAN MUSEUM OF ART

FIGURE
16

FIGURE
17

Spanish main gauche *at the peak of its development, about 1640–1650.*

THE METROPOLITAN MUSEUM OF ART

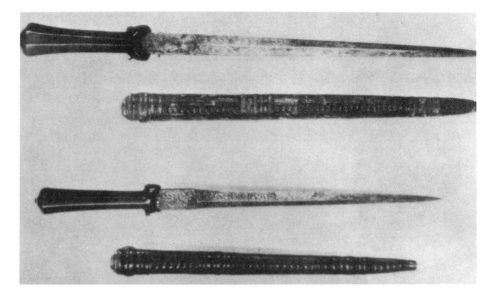

FIGURE
18

English kidney daggers with wooden hilts. The top specimen is dated 1620. It is supposed to have belonged to Col. Blood, who attempted to steal the crown jewels in 1671. Both blades bear gilt-etched decorations. Crown copyright photograph reproduced by permission of the Controller of Her Britannic Majesty's Stationery Office.

H. M. TOWER OF LONDON

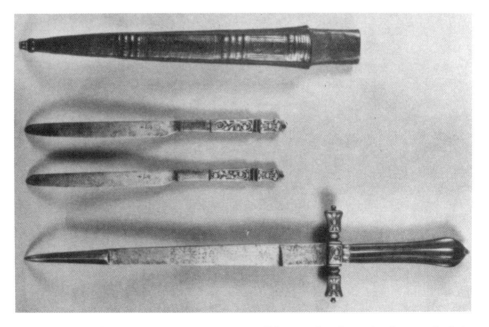

FIGURE
19

English quillon dagger with accompanying small knives dated 1624. The guard of the dagger and the grips of the small knives are inlaid with silver.

JOHN HAYWARD COLLECTION

was the specific form of dagger indicated. One knife has survived which belonged to one of the Pilgrims at Plymouth, but it is a table knife, and as far as is known there is no other existing knife that can be traced to the English colonies. Even at Jamestown, where National Park Service archaeologists have uncovered numerous weapons, no daggers have been found. The only surviving blades have been from butcher knives.

FIGURE
20

Knife blades excavated at Jamestown. The larger blade is 16 inches long. Both have forged bolsters.   NATIONAL PARK SERVICE

After 1650, however, one form of dagger is easily distinguished in America. This was the plug bayonet. The concept of this new arm was simple. The standard dagger blade of the period was fitted with tapering wooden grips which could be forced into the muzzle of a musket. As obvious as this device might seem, it was a revolutionary development in the arms field. Before its advent a gun that had been discharged was useless, and the soldier usually either dropped it and drew his sword for hand-to-hand work or retreated behind a company of pikemen who offered him protection while he reloaded. With the new bayonet the empty musket could be converted into a sort of pike, and the musketeer could hold his own against a charging enemy armed with swords or spears. Also, when not in use on the gun, the bayonet was as handy as the dagger or general utility knife that the soldier had previously been accustomed to wear.

The plug bayonet was developed in Europe early in the seventeenth century, but it apparently did not reach America until after 1650. The earliest known specimen used here is of French manufacture. It was taken from one of France's Indian allies near Deerfield, Massachusetts, in 1675, and is illustrated in the chapter on Indian knives.

Since these knives were so simple, many of them were produced in America during succeeding years. Sometimes blades were specially forged for the purpose, but more often old sword blades were cut down and fitted with new hilts. Usually there was only a rudimentary guard consisting of an oval plate of brass or iron, and the grips were turned simply from American woods, primarily walnut, maple or cherry. In Europe there was normally a globular swelling at the base of the grips which afforded a better hold when withdrawing the bayonet from the gun muzzle. In American specimens this feature was often omitted.

The plug bayonet remained popular until about 1700. Thereafter it rapidly disappeared as it was replaced by the socket bayonet. The new bayonet was more efficient when on the musket but less useful as a knife, and so it was necessary for the average soldier to go back to the practice of carrying a separate knife once more. It was not until the appearance of the Dahlgren bayonet in the 1860's that America once more saw a combination knife and bayonet that was really useful both ways.

Although the eighteenth century witnessed the passing of the plug bayonet, it also brought to America some new and very interesting knives. These included the Scottish dirk, the rifleman's knife, a further development of the dagger, and the pocketknife.

Scots began coming to America in some numbers shortly after 1700, many of them settling in the southern colonies. In the 1730's and '40's there was a Highland Independent Company at Darien, Georgia, which served with General Oglethorpe's Regiment and took part in the battle of the Bloody Marsh against the Spanish. After the defeat of Bonnie Prince Charlie's cause in 1745 many Scots who had fought the English with him left their homes and came to America, large numbers settling in Scottish communities in the Carolinas. Several Scottish regiments fought here during the French and Indian War, Pontiac's Conspiracy and the Revolution. The most outstanding was the 42nd Regiment or Black Watch which won the respect of American troops by its gallantry in the suicidal attack at Fort Ticonderoga in 1758 and later in its heroic efforts at the Battle of Bushy Run, which broke Pontiac's siege of Pittsburgh and saved the defenders. During the Revolution several Scottish regiments fought with the British Army. The Black Watch returned. With it came the 71st or Frazier's Highlanders, the 80th or Royal Edinburgh Volunteers and the 84th or Royal Highland Emigrants.

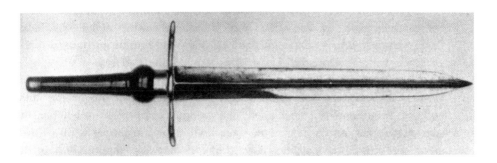

Late 17th-century European plug bayonet.   AUTHOR'S COLLECTION

FIGURE
21

FIGURE
22

American-made plug bayonet, late 17th Century or early 18th century.
BENJAMIN F. HUBBELL COLLECTION

The Scot carried two typical knives, the dirk and the *sgian dubh*. The *sgian dubh* was a small knife, often with a curved blade and a wooden handle without a guard. Originally it was carried concealed under the armpit. Later it was worn in the stocking. The dirk was a large all-purpose knife equally useful for meals or battle. It was worn in a scabbard at the front of the belt.

The Scottish dirk was a regional variation of the kidney dagger previously described. It seems to have developed as a special type during the seventeenth century, though surviving specimens that were made before 1700 are excessively rare today. By the 1730's and '40's when the Scots were coming to America in large numbers, the usual dirk had a wooden hilt deeply carved with interlacing strapwork. The grips were short, terminating in haunches over the base of the blade which were reminiscent of the kidney daggers' lobes. The pommel was a flat cap. Usually there was a plate of brass, pewter or silver on the pommel and at the base of the haunches. Occasional specimens with bone or metal hits are found, however. The blade was straight, single-edged and triangular in cross section. Sometimes there was a fuller or even piercings at the back. Quite frequently, especially after 1745, these blades were made from old sword blades.

These dirks were carried in leather sheaths mounted in metal to match the pommel plates of the hilts. Often the sheaths were tooled with interlacing straps similar to those on the hilt. A special feature on some was the provision for an extra small knife or two or a knife and fork.

During the second half of the eighteenth century, the Scottish dirk lost much of its simplicity and good design. The grips became longer and more bulbous, sometimes thistle-shaped The pommel thickened until it became almost globular. At the very end, after 1800, it was often set with a cairngorm and tilted on its side. The strapwork carving deteriorated as the interlacing bands became wider and the grooves shallower. The haunches became deeper, and terminated in a straight line across the blade instead of the crescent which was characteristic of the earlier specimens.

FIGURE
23

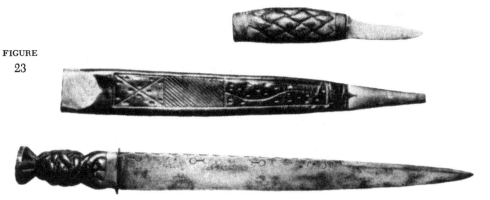

Early 18th-century Scottish dirk and sgian dubh. ROYAL SCOTTISH MUSEUM, EDINBURGH

FIGURE
24

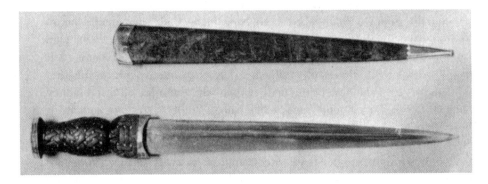

Scottish silver-mounted dirk, about 1775. This dirk belonged to Capt. Angus McDonald of the 84th Regiment, which was raised in 1775 for service in the American Revolution and disbanded in 1784. Crown copyright photograph reproduced by permission of the Controller of Her Britannic Majesty's Stationery Office.

SCOTTISH UNITED SERVICES MUSEUM, EDINBURGH

Meanwhile, in America, another very interesting type of figure was developing with a set of knives all his own. This was the frontiersman, the backwoods settler or hunter. In the early 1700's the Eastern Seaboard had already become a highly settled area with large towns and cities and relatively good roads. It was no longer necessary for the average citizen to carry a knife as a weapon. Thus, except for an occasional hunting trip, he normally carried only a folding pocketknife of one of two types described later in the chapter on pocketknives. Even when these same men joined the American army during the Revolution, the only knife they carried was usually the jackknife.

On the frontier, however, the situation was entirely different. There was almost constant danger of Indian raids. Hunting and trapping and primitive conditions made a large knife a constant necessity. Often standard carving or kitchen knives were fitted with a sheath, but many homemade knives also were produced.

The typical knife made by one of these backwoodsmen was a simple sturdy affair. Sometimes the blade was roughly forged by a local blacksmith. Sometimes it was ground out of an old file. The handle might be fashioned from wood, but one of the most popular materials was deer antler. Handmade knives of the cruder type change very little, and thus it is impossible to distinguish an eighteenth-century knife from one made one hundred years later unless a datable manufactured product has been used in its construction.

Frontiersmen of all description carried these large knives in their belts everywhere they went. They were as much a mark of their occupation as the fringed hunting shirts they wore. Residents of the big Eastern cities noted and spoke with awe of these "butcher" or "scalping" knives carried by the backwoods rifle companies during the Revolution.

Among these frontiersmen the riflemen were a special group. Rifles as well as the commoner smooth-bore guns had been used in Europe for centuries, and some of the colonists brought rifled guns to America with them. They were particularly popular among the German, Swiss and Swedish settlers of Pennsylvania who developed the European rifle into the well-known American or "Kentucky" rifle. Rifles relied for their accuracy on a ball that fitted the bore tightly and thus would take the spin imparted by the rifle grooves. This tight fit was achieved by wrapping the ball in a greased patch of cloth before it was rammed down the barrel.

Sometimes a rifleman had his patches cut in advance, but at other times he had to trim them as he loaded his gun. Then he needed a knife. The big "scalping" knife in his belt could be used for this purpose, but often he carried a smaller, handier knife in or attached to his rifle bag. These rifle knives were made in a great variety of patterns. Usually the blade was three or four inches long, and the handle might be wood, antler or even cow horn. The early ones were unusually crude and unattractive. In the nineteenth century some handsome rifle knives with inlaid hilts were made by gunsmiths to match the decoration of the rifle.

FIGURE
25

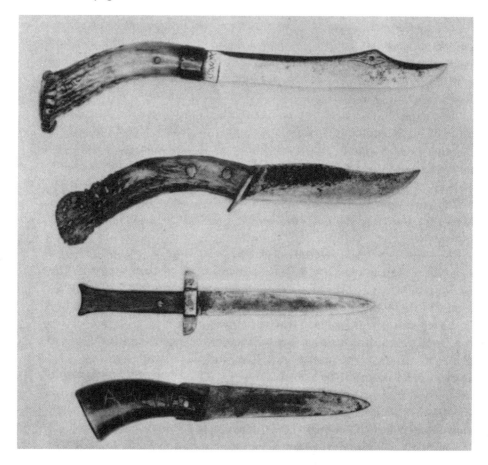

A selection of American rifle knives with grips of antler, wood and horn and blades fashioned from files, saws or specially forged. The top specimen is definitely 18th century. The others were probably made after 1800, but the same shapes had been used long before.

HERB GLASS, LEON C. JACKSON, CARL PIPPERT AND JOSEPH AIKEN COLLECTIONS

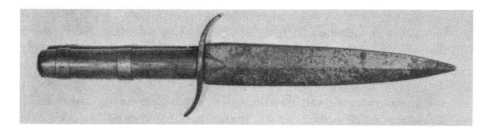

FIGURE
26

Simple American dagger with 6¾-inch blade, iron guard and wooden grips bound with pewter bands.   LEONARD D. PELTON COLLECTION

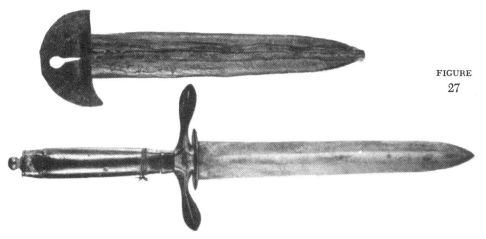

FIGURE
27

Dagger with 6½-inch blade carried by Capt. William Walton of the North Carolina line in the Revolution. The grips are wood; the guard and pommel, gilded brass.
U. S. NATIONAL MUSEUM

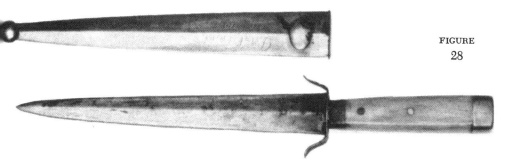

FIGURE
28

*American silver-mounted dagger with bone grips and a 6⅛-inch blade. The scabbard is engraved "*DON'T TREAD ON ME.*" The quillons have been bent.*
HERB GLASS COLLECTION

As was noted above, the backwoodsman carried his scalping knife with him when he marched off to fight in the Revolution, while the private in the regular regiments carried a pocketknife. There was also one other knife that saw some use in the Revolution, particularly by officers: the dagger. Both the rifleman's "scalping" knife and the private's jackknife are mentioned in regulations. The dagger was strictly unofficial, carried only at the whim of the individual, and its existence is evidenced only by a few surviving specimens. Judging by these, they were not large weapons. The blades were about six inches long and double-edged. The guards were usually simple cross quillons. The known specimens run the gamut from simple hand forgings to fine silver mounts. None could have been a real fighting weapon, but they could have served as a last defense in an emergency.

These were the principal knives used during the first eight centuries of American history. The next 175 years brought a vastly greater variety and an infinitely larger production. The successors to the pioneer types must be considered separately and at greater length.

THE BOWIE AND ITS ASSOCIATES

FIGURE
30

James Bowie   BEN PALMER COLLECTION   *Rezin P. Bowie*

IN THE history of American arms three weapons stand out above all the rest: the Kentucky rifle, the Colt revolver and the bowie knife. Each was a superb weapon, but more than that, each became so much a part of the American scene that it transcended its role in history and became a part of the great American legend.

Of none is this truer than the bowie knife. A century ago European visitors who ventured beyond the Appalachians found it such an integral part of the American way of life that they felt compelled to comment on it at length in accounts of their adventures. Schools were established in most of the larger cities of the old Southwest to teach its use. In many communities no man, whether hunter, gambler, tradesman or political leader felt himself fully clothed without one. It gave its name to the state

25

where it was born, and Arkansas has been known unofficially ever since as the Bowie State. Even today the mere mention of its name immediately conjures up a picture of a wild and rough era characterized by violence and sudden death.

Among collectors and students of knives there is no more magic name than "bowie knife." All agree that a bowie is a most desirable knife to own, but ask them exactly what a bowie is, and agreement ends. Some maintain that it is a sheath knife with a clipped point. Any knife, no matter what its size, can qualify. Others insist that only large fighting knives with clipped points can qualify. A third group feels that the shape of the point is immaterial as long as it is a large knife; and a final group is willing to classify all of the various sheath knives of the period from 1830 to 1890 as bowies.

The problem is not simple. Each faction has some justification for its opinion. Certainly the original knife made for James Bowie was a large heavy knife suitable for both self-defense and general utility in the woods. It was single-edged with a false edge at the back of the point permitting a backstroke in fighting. The record is not absolutely clear, but it seems probable that the point was clipped. Thus it would seem that in its purest form the term should apply to large knives with clipped points. It should also be noted, however, that within a decade after the original knife was made, the name was being applied to all sheath knives large enough for use as weapons. This continued for the next thirty or forty years and covered the period of the knife's greatest popularity. The argument of contemporary usage plus the fact that one cannot be absolutely certain that Bowie's original knife had a clipped point provide good grounds for blanketing in all single-edged sheath knives of the period. The matter of size, too, is ephemeral. Everyone would agree that a blade of nine inches or more would qualify a knife as a weapon. But what about six inches? Modern American military knives are only a fraction longer, and a man can be killed with far less.

In view of this situation and of the conflicting definitions, it would seem best to establish how the term will be used here. The bowie in its purest form will be considered a large knife with a clipped point. Other knives of the period will also be classed as bowies but with qualifications describing either the point, the size or any other feature that causes them to vary from the pure form.

The story of this fabulous knife began in 1830. It was made in that

FIGURE
31

The classical bowie in its purest form. It is a massive hand-forged weapon with a 13¾-inch blade, 2⅜ inches wide. The mountings are iron, and there is a brass strip on the back of the blade. The only marks are crudely engraved stars on the quillon terminals.
WILLIAM O. SWEET COLLECTION

year, possibly by an Arkansas blacksmith named James Black, for the legendary James Bowie. So much legend surrounds Bowie, in fact, that it is often impossible at this date to distinguish fact from fancy. The romantic tales of Bowie's prowess had such an effect on the popularity of the knife, even in his own time, that it really makes little difference whether they are true or not. Bowie was probably born in Logan County, Kentucky, April 10, 1796. He grew to be a large man, six feet tall, weighing some 180 pounds. He was an open-hearted son of the frontier, generous to a fault and a true gentleman. But even his brother admitted he had a terrible temper. His career was varied and noteworthy, ranging from lumbering to the slave trade and land speculation. He prospered in all and built a considerable fortune. During the late 1820's he became interested in Texas, married there and was granted provisional citizenship by the Mexican government in 1830. When the movement for Texas independence began, Bowie took an active part and was appointed a colonel in the Texas Army. He commanded the forces at the Alamo and died there with the rest of the garrison, March 8, 1836.

The direct antecedent of the bowie knife was made for Rezin P. Bowie, James's brother. According to Rezin himself, he personally designed a knife 9¼ inches long and 1½ inches wide for use in hunting. It was single-edged and had a straight blade. In 1827 he gave this knife to James, who had recently been shot while unarmed by Major Norris Wright, in the thought that he might need it for self-protection. A short time later Bowie did indeed use the knife in the famous Vidalia Sandbar fight. After being shot in the

FIGURE
32

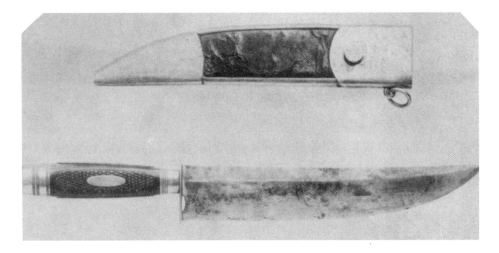

Early bowie knife made by Searles of Baton Rouge for Rezin P. Bowie. Rezin had a number of these made for presentation to friends. He gave this one to H. W. Fowler of the U. S. Dragoons. From a glass negative found in the effects of Col. Washington Bowie.   BEN PALMER COLLECTION

hip and stabbed in the chest with a sword cane, Bowie, according to a friendly report, killed Wright with the knife and then, after receiving another pistol ball in his left arm, wounded a second antagonist, one Alfred Blanchard, and caused him to flee the sandbar. In 1829 Bowie also is said to have fought a notorious Natchez gambler named John Sturdivant, who had cheated the son of one of his friends. In this encounter the left wrist of the fighters were tied together with a scarf. Sturdivant tried an attack. Bowie parried and slashed his enemy's knife arm, severing the tendons and rendering him helpless. Always a magnanimous victor, Bowie refrained from killing Sturdivant.

Shortly thereafter Bowie went to Texas. On his return with provisional citizenship in 1830, he is purported to have visited the shop of James Black and asked him to make a knife according to a pattern he had devised. Apparently this pattern was based on the knife he had received from Rezin and which had served him so well in his previous encounters.

Black, in later life, always maintained that he had improved on Bowie's model and thus had really invented the Bowie knife himself. As far as can be determined, Bowie had altered Rezin's knife by increasing its size. Black may have added the false edge at the point if, indeed, he actually made the knife at all.

Shortly after Bowie received his new knife, word spread of a new battle, and this started the knife on its way to fame. Although Bowie had spared Sturdivant's life in the knife duel at Natchez-under-the-Hill, the gambler never forgave him. Instead of being grateful, the story goes, he hired three ruffians to kill Bowie. These desperadoes ambushed James on his return trip to Texas and rushed him, knives in hand. With his new knife Bowie struck off the head of the assassin who seized his bridle. Then, despite a stab wound in the calf, he dismounted and disemboweled the second. The third turned and fled, but Bowie caught him and split his head in two. Word of this feat spread rapidly. Bowie, already noted for his achievements with the weapon, became the prototype of all knife fighters, and quantities of new knives were made or reputedly made in the image of Bowie's. The era of the bowie knife had begun.

The West of Bowie's day provided the perfect environment for the development of the knife cult. The lawless element prevalent in all frontier areas, the rough and violent river men and the plentiful gamblers all found the knife a handy weapon that could be carried inconspicuously and used quietly. The law-abiding citizens needed the knife for protection and for the defense of their frequently over-sensitive honor. The day of the civilian sword had passed. Instead the well-equipped gentleman carried a pistol in his pocket and a knife beneath his coattails.

Hundreds of incidents involving knives were recorded in the newspapers of the day. They ran the gamut from nefarious murders through the settling of violent quarrels and affairs of honor to the saving of lives and virtue from attacking beasts and desperadoes. There were brawls in taverns and gambling houses, on river boats, in the streets and even in state legislatures, all of them settled by knives.

One incident, far less sanguinary than most, involved the U. S. House of Representatives itself. Congressional tempers were short in the spring of 1860. The impending crisis of the Civil War dominated all else, and the air was tense. There were individual fist fights between members, general brawls, duels and challenges to duels. One of the recently seated members was John Fox Potter of Wisconsin. Potter had a reputation in his home state as a mild and gentle man, but his actions in Congress scarcely support it.

FIGURE
33

The knives of "Bowie Knife" Potter. According to family tradition, the top knife with an 11½-inch blade by R. E. Hardy of Sheffield is the one he planned to use in his duel with Pryor. The specimen at the lower left is a Wostenholm with a 5½-inch blade. In the lower right is one of the trophies which were showered on Potter. It is an American-made knife, and the plate on the grips states that it was captured from one of the Louisiana Tigers at Norfolk in 1862 and presented to Potter on behalf of Brig. Gen. Viele, May 31, 1862.

WISCONSIN STATE HISTORICAL SOCIETY

He had hardly taken his seat before he was engaged in a fist fight on the aisle during which he captured the wig of a representative from Mississippi, received a black eye in return and was challenged to a duel.

Mutual friends patched up that dispute, but another soon followed. On April 8, 1860, a group of Southerners led by Roger A. Pryor of Virginia tried to silence Owen Lovejoy of Illinois during one of his virulent denunciations of slavery. Potter and others sprang to Lovejoy's defense. The sergeant at arms parted the two groups before the affair had passed beyond mutual insults. Shortly thereafter, when the official record appeared, it stated that Potter had shouted, "This side shall be heard, let the consequences be what they may!" Pryor accused the Wisconsin representative of having composed this statement and inserted it after the event. Words were exchanged, and Pryor's seconds waited on Potter.

In response Potter issued as bizarre a set of conditions as was ever placed before a Southern gentleman schooled in the *code duello* as it was practiced in the East. He declared that he was glad to oblige the offended Virginian and would be pleased to meet him at his convenience in a closed room with bowie knives of equal weight and length of blade, the fight to continue until one of the participants fell, and Potter added that he "would endeavor to carve him [Pryor] so skillfully as forever to remove his desire for fight." Pryor did not learn of the terms until much later. His seconds declined for him immediately upon receipt of Potter's message on the grounds that the proposal was barbarous and ungentlemanly. Another duel was then narrowly avoided when Potter's second thought that the terms of the refusal reflected on his own honor.

The newspapers seized upon the affair with avidity. It became a featured story throughout the country, and Potter became a national figure. Republicans lauded him as a hero while Democrats excoriated him as a "braggart fool." Knives were showered on him from all parts of the country, some bearing the names of persons on whom the donors wished them used. The Republicans of the State of Missouri presented him with a seven-foot knife bearing the punning inscription, "I will always keep a Prior engagement," and for the rest of his life he was known as "Bowie Knife" Potter.

The Potter incident is of no great importance in itself. Its main interest lies in the fact that it involved members of Congress and that it illustrates the knife's hold on the popular imagination thirty years after its first appearance.

Popular opinion of the bowie knife had not been static during these thirty years. Early newspaper accounts seem to dwell with a perverted pride on gory tales of knife-fighting. Then the public tired of the novelty, and a feeling of revulsion set in. From 1837 to 1839 Tennessee, Alabama and Mississippi passed stringent laws covering the use, transfer or even public handling of such knives. Despite these acts, however, the bowie retained much of its appeal, and it was carried as widely as before. During the Mexican War it was a popular though unofficial side arm of American troops. It played an important part in the violence in Kansas and Missouri in the 1850's, and many soldiers on both sides carried it into the Civil War.

So much for the general background of the bowie; what did the knife itself look like? The earliest specimens were those made in America by local smiths supposedly copying Bowie's original. These were large knives with heavy blades nine to fifteen inches long and one and a half to two inches wide. They were thick enough to give the blade sufficient rigidity to lop off saplings, split the skull of a bear or a human adversary, joint game, or dig in rough ground. The blades were usually well made but lacked the high finish of later and imported products. The guard was normally a simple cross often with S-curved quillons or a plate of iron or brass, and the grips were commonly wood, antler or bone. There were almost never any marks or inscriptions. On a few of the blacksmith-made knives there was also a most interesting feature. This was a hardened strip of brass along the back of the blade, apparently designed to catch the edge of an opponent's on a parry and prevent the possibility of its sliding up past the guard and injuring the hand. Knives with this strip are excessively rare today. It is only found on American blades, never on British specimens. The typical hand-forged knives, however, are not so scarce. They were made all along the frontier, starting probably within a few weeks after the original was made and continuing at least until the end of the Civil War, thirty-five years later.

FIGURE
34

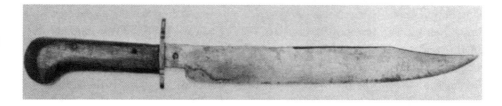

Crude American bowie made from a file. The guard is iron. The 12¾-inch blade is swaged but has no real false edge. It might possibly be Confederate.

LEON C. JACKSON COLLECTION

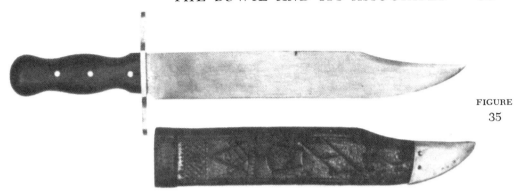

FIGURE
35

American bowie with 12⅛-inch blade and brass mounts. Again, the blade is swaged but has no real false edge. The scabbard is tooled with Masonic emblems, a fouled anchor and other devices. WILLIAM SHEMERLUK COLLECTION

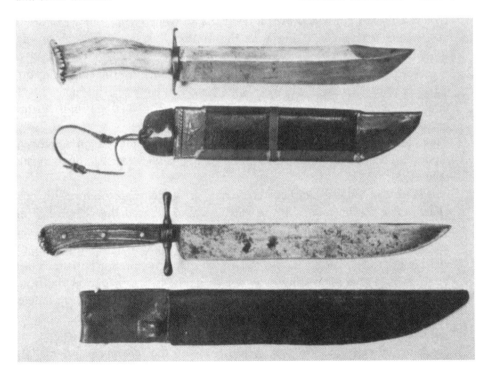

FIGURE
36

Two American-made bowies. The upper specimen has a heavy 9¾-inch blade with a high median ridge. The mounts of the scabbard are tinned iron. It was found in Texas with a tradition of Confederate use. The lower knife has two unusual features. It was forged with a bolster like a carving knife, and the iron guard was passed through the bolster. The sheath has an interesting leather lug designed to hold the knife in place. LEON C. JACKSON COLLECTION

It was not long, however, before the English cutlery industry took note of the demand for these knives. George Wostenholm, founder of the Washington Works in Sheffield, had a representative in New York in 1830 and made personal visits to the United States himself in 1836 and after to study the demand and the market. Wostenholm probably made more bowie knives for the American trade than any other firm, and he made some of the best. His trade mark of I*XL became a standard of quality and was accorded the sincere praise of imitation by other English cutlers who approached it as closely as they dared with such variants as XLNT, I*XCD, NON*XL and the like. Ranging behind Wostenholm came the Sheffield firms of Joseph Rodgers & Sons, Edward Barnes, and Alexander. After these came a whole host of others. Some of these endeavored to add appeal to their wares by marking blades and scabbards with the letters U S separated by a star or N Y separated by a federal shield. None of them, however, had any official connection either with the United States government or the State of New York.

American firms apparently did not manufacture bowie knives in any quantity until after the Civil War. Some concerns, however, did have knives made for them in England which bore their names. Thus one finds blades marked "Manufactured by W. & S. Butcher for Graveley & Wreaks, New York" or "E. K. Tryon Co., Phila, Pa., Made in England." Such American names as do appear on bowies prior to the Civil War usually indicate dealers.

With the English imports came the great diversity of forms which characterize the secondary bowie knives. Some followed the classical form with large blades and clipped points. Others introduced the symmetrical spear point; and still others, the slanted point in which the back angles sharply to meet the edge. Blades ran all sizes from fourteen or fifteen inches to six inches. One interesting evolution to notice is the change in the false edge from a sharp cutting surface to a vestigial swage. On the early knives the false edge was always sharp. As time wore on it became a bevel only, left unsharpened. The presence of a sharp false edge is not always an absolute indication of an early knife. Some of the late ones also had it, particularly among the American-made knives of the Civil War period.

Hilts also developed variety. German silver, white brass, coin and sterling silver joined the metals used for mountings. These usually consisted of a guard, a ferrule at the base of the grips, sometimes an escutcheon plate

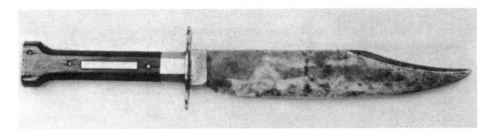

FIGURE
37

Early Sheffield bowie, about 1836, made by W. Butcher. The blade is 8¾ inches long.
The mountings are German silver. BEN PALMER COLLECTION

FIGURE
38

Sheffield bowie knife made by George Wostenholm about 1836–1840. Its 9-inch blade
is very similar to that on the one made for Rezin Bowie. The grips are bone; the mounts,
German silver. BEN PALMER COLLECTION

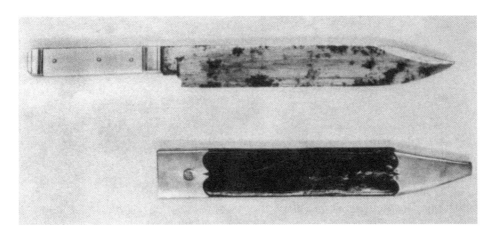

FIGURE
39

Sheffield bowie, about 1840, without guard. The 9½-inch blade has a semiclipped point.
The grips are bone; the mounts, German silver. BEN PALMER COLLECTION

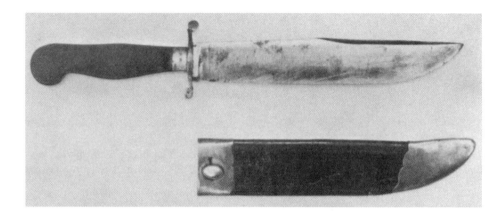

FIGURE
40

American bowie by Reinhardt of Baltimore, about 1840. The blade is 9½ inches long, and the grips are wood. The knife itself is mounted in iron, but the sheath mounts are coin silver.   BEN PALMER COLLECTION

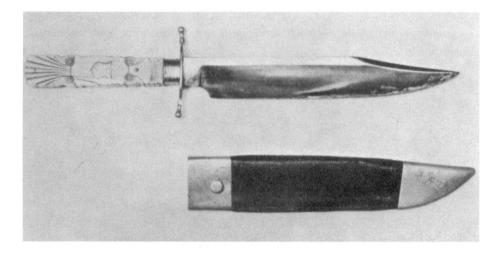

FIGURE
41

Bowie knife about 1840–50 by Alfred Hunter, probably of Sheffield. The blade is 8⅞ inches long. The grips are bone; the mountings, German silver.

BEN PALMER COLLECTION

FIGURE
42

Slightly later bowie by Butcher, about 1840–45. A very unusual feature on this knife is the folding corkscrew in the handle. The blade is 8⅞ inches long. The grips are bone; the mounts, German silver.   BEN PALMER COLLECTION

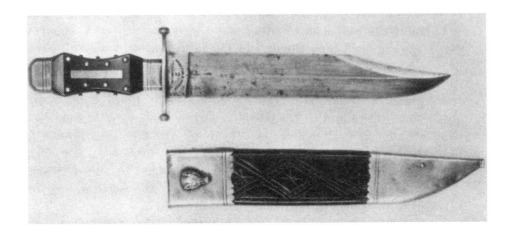

FIGURE
43

*Bowie made about 1845–1850 marked "*Sheffield Works/2/Philadelphia*." Little is known about the history of this knife, but several identical specimens exist. The blade is 10 inches long. The grips are wood, and the mounts are brass.*

BEN PALMER COLLECTION

on the reverse of the grips and a cap or pommel at the butt end. Grips were made in both one and two pieces from wood, mother-of-pearl, horn, antler, bone, ivory, tortoise shell and German silver.

Along with variations in shapes and materials came the innovation of blade decoration. Usually these decorations were acid etched on the metal and left bright. Occasional specimens using bluing and gilding to accent the etching are known, and some late specimens used a gilt background with the etched designs bright.

Most of these decorations involved patriotic motifs and slogans. It is interesting to note the jingoism of some of these English etched sayings conceived to capture the fancy of prospective American buyers. It is difficult to set up a chronology for these slogans since some persisted from the 1840's through the Civil War. Generally speaking, however, one does note a certain time element. In the 1840's one finds such sayings as "An American Asks for Nothing but what is Right and Submits to Nothing that is Wrong." After the discovery of gold in California this is frequently changed to read a Californian instead of an American, and it is coupled with such comments as "I can dig Gold from Quartz." In the 1850's and early 1860's another phrase is sometimes added: "America, the Land of the Free and the Home of the Brave, Protected by her Noble and Brave Volunteers." During this same period one also finds "The American's Pride, Equal Laws, Equal Rights and Justice to All." The mounting slavery controversy brought such diametrically opposed mottoes as "Death to Abolition" and "Death to Traitors." In addition to these bombastic sayings, there were also many more prosaic legends such as "The Californian Knife," "A Sure Defense," "Self-Defender," "The American Hunting Knife," "The Genuine Arkansas Toothpick," "For Stags & Buffaloes," and many others.

Some blades bore stamped designs instead of etched ones. Among these are found sphinxes, mounted hunters, dogs, deer, lions, unicorns, Maltese crosses and the like, with such words as "Try Me," "The Hunter's Companion," "I Surpass All," "Alabama Hunting Knife" and references to General Zachary Taylor's victory at Buena Vista.

Hilts were also decorated. Some were copied from table cutlery with shells and scrollwork and made entirely of German silver. There were also pommels shaped like horses' heads or shells, and embossed representations of the legendary half-horse half-alligator creation of the Kentucky riflemen. Finally there were state crests and patriotic motifs, including eagles, flags, federal shields and the motto "Liberty."

FIGURE
44

Sheffield bowie made for an American dealer. The 6-inch blade is stamped "E. K. TRYON Co./PHIL PA/MADE IN ENGLAND." It was carried by a naval officer in the Mexican War.

U. S. NATIONAL MUSEUM

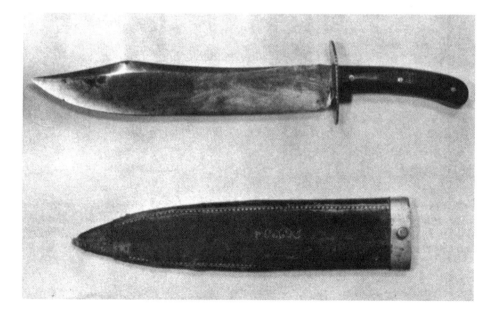

FIGURE
45

American bowie marked "SOMMIS/PROVIDENCE," about 1850. This may have been made in England for Sommis, but aside from the scabbard, the general appearance indicates American workmanship.   THEODORE GOLDENBERG COLLECTION

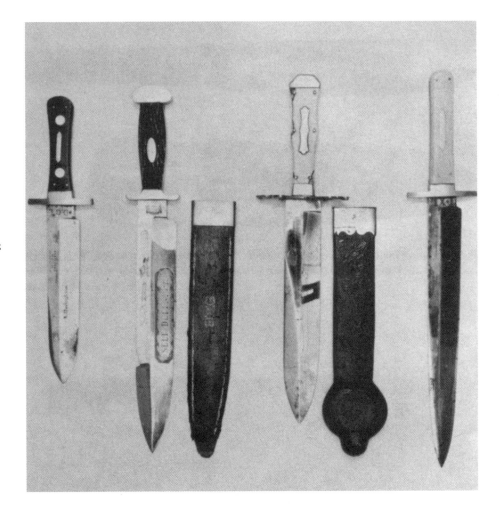

FIGURE
46

Group of single-edged Sheffield bowies with spear points. All are mounted in German silver, and blades range from 7⅛ to 10¾ inches. From top to bottom the makers are Wilson Swift, Wragg & Sons, James Rodgers, and G. Wostenholm & Son. Note the notch in the back of the blade of the second knife.   HERB GLASS COLLECTION

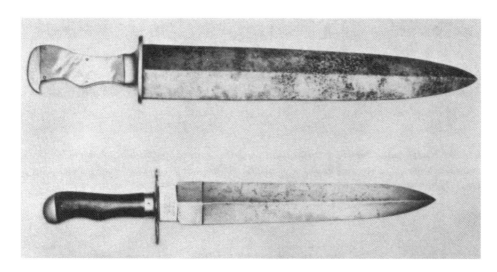

FIGURE
47

Two double-edged bowies with spear points. The upper specimen with a 14½-inch blade and pearl grips is probably American-made. The lower knife with a 12-inch blade was made by Geo. Wostenholm & Co. about 1850–55. The blade was originally etched "GEO. WOSTENHOLM & CO'S. CELEBRATED CALIFORNIA KNIFE."

HERB GLASS COLLECTION

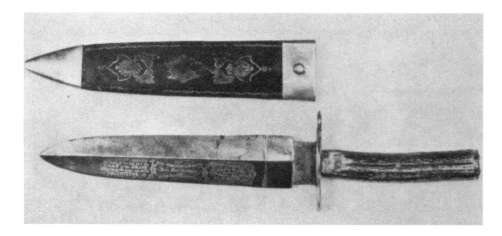

FIGURE
48

Double-edged bowie with spear point made by George Wostenholm & Son about 1850–55. The 9¾-inch blade is blued and decorated with gilt etching. The mounts are German silver, and the sheath has a green leather veneer.   HARRY D. BERRY, JR. COLLECTION

FIGURE
49

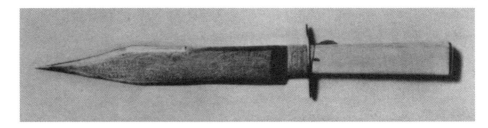

Sheffield bowie made by H. Y. Wilkinson & Co. about 1855–60. The 8¼-inch blade is decorated with an eagle and mottoes in bright etching. The grips are ivory; the mountings, German silver. ROBERT ABELS COLLECTION

FIGURE
50

Sheffield bowie by George Wostenholm & Son made for Southern sympathizers about 1850–60. The 8¼-inch blade is etched "DEATH TO ABOLITION" in large letters. The grips are checkered ebony; the mounts, German silver. ROBERT ABELS COLLECTION

FIGURE
51

Sheffield bowie made for an American firm. The 11⅞-inch blade is marked "W&S BUTCHER FOR GRAVELY & WREAKS/NEW YORK." The grips are tortoise shell, the mounts, German silver, and the sheath has a red leather veneer.

NORMAN TAPLEY COLLECTION

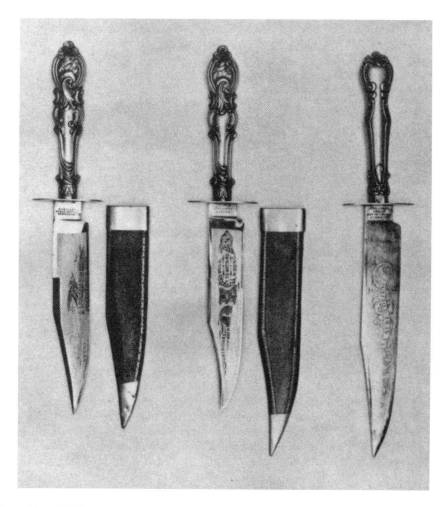

FIGURE
52

Three Sheffield bowies of 1850–60 with etched blades and table-cutlery handles of German silver. The blades range from 6½ to 8 inches. From left to right the makers are G. Woodhead, Manson, and S. C. Wraht (?). The last name is somewhat illegible.

HERB GLASS COLLECTION

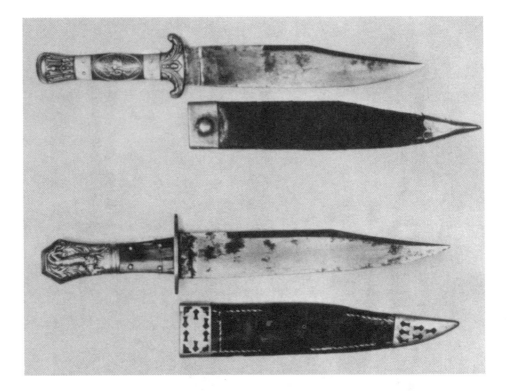

FIGURE
53

Sheffield bowies with decorated pommels, 1850–60. The upper specimen by John Klin-gard has a 6-inch blade, pearl grips and embossed German silver mounts. The lower knife, by Woodhead & Hartley, has a 7¾-inch blade, tortoise-shell grips and a German silver pommel embossed with the mythical half horse-half alligator. The reverse side of the blade is also etched with mottoes.   ROBERT ABELS COLLECTION

FIGURE
54

Sheffield bowie by James Westa, about 1860, with a version of the Louisiana state arms on the pommel. The blade is 7¾ inches long; the grips, horn; and the mounts, German silver.   CARL PIPPERT COLLECTION

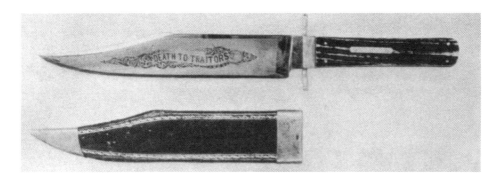

FIGURE
55

Sheffield bowie made by W. & H. Whitehead about 1860 to appeal to Union sentiment. The 8-inch blade is etched "DEATH TO TRAITORS." The mountings are German silver; the grips, antler; and the sheath has a maroon leather veneer. HERB GLASS COLLECTION

This is only a sampling of the commoner decorative devices. Where individual taste and craftsmanship are concerned, the possibilities are always limitless.

The scabbards in which bowie knives were worn throughout the nineteenth century varied according to where the knives were made. American knives usually had sheaths of harness leather, plain but sturdy. Some had belt loops, some studs, and some frogs for attachment to the belt. The English sheaths were most often made of pressed paper or cardboard with a thin leather veneer. They were handsome with gilt tooling, designs and sometimes mottoes. The leather veneer itself was usually colored in one of a variety of hues. Red, green, blue, purple, yellow and golden brown were all popular. The pressed paper would not stand up in service, however. A good soaking in a heavy rain or two or even the effects of continued contact with perspiration caused the pretty scabbards to disintegrate. Then the owner had to seek out the local saddler or cobbler and have a more practical sheath made.

Almost all English sheaths and most American ones had metal throats and tips. These were usually made of German silver, brass, tin or iron. As a rule they were of the same metal as the mountings of the knife itself. The tip prevented the point of the blade from cutting through the sheath and accidentally stabbing the wearer or tearing his clothes. The throat reinforced the opening and helped the sheath hold its shape. Usually the throat had a button on the obverse side which caught over the belt when the knife was thrust beneath it and so helped hold it in position.

FIGURE
56

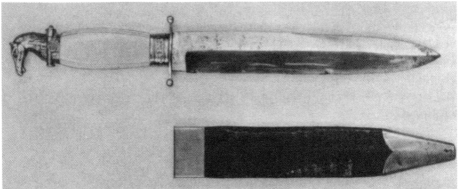

Group of Sheffield bowies with horse-head pommels showing some of the variations in shape and size. Blades range from 8½ to 12⅞ inches. All are mounted in German silver. From top to bottom the makers are W. C. Reaves, R. Bunting & Sons, Fenton & Shore, and Ibbotson Peace & Co.   ROBERT ABELS AND BEN PALMER COLLECTIONS

FIGURE
57

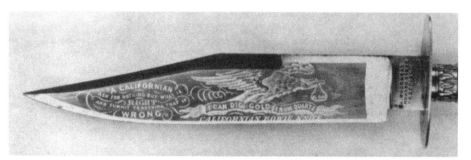

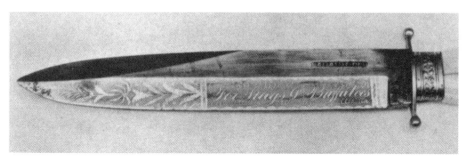

Details of blade etching. From top to bottom these are from the knives illustrated in figures 48, 55, 52 and 56.

FIGURE
58

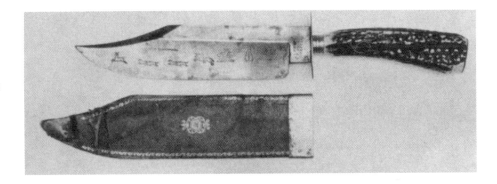

Sheffield bowie by W. F. Jackson with stamped decorations. The 8⅞-inch blade is exceptionally wide and heavy. The mounts are German silver.

WILLIAM SHEMERLUK COLLECTION

FIGURE
59

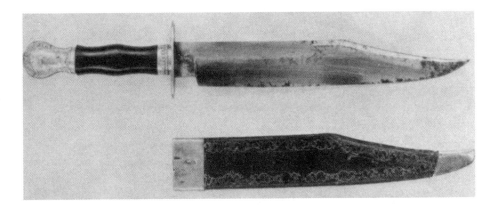

Sheffield bowie by James Walters & Co. with decorated pommel. The blade is 11⅞ inches long. The grips are wood, and the mountings, German silver.

BEN PALMER COLLECTION

FIGURE
60

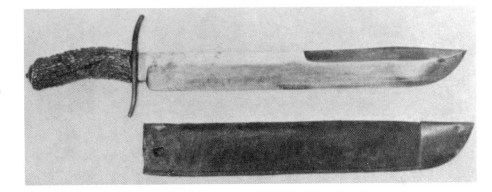

Huge American bowie by Reinhardt with a blade 17¾ inches long. The grips are antler; the mountings, iron.

BEN PALMER COLLECTION

The Civil War made the bowie as popular on the East Coast as it had been west of the Appalachians. Almost every volunteer on both sides wore one. The town of Ashby, Massachusetts, for instance, presented every one of its residents with a bowie knife when he enlisted, as did Shelburne Falls and many other Massachusetts towns, while Company C of the 1st Georgia Infantry from Cass County were known as "The Bowie Knife Boys." Veterans recalled, however, that the knives were soon abandoned, especially by Union soldiers who found that their issued weapons were sufficient and that they had enough to carry without them. Confederate soldiers were not so well armed, and therefore the big knives remained more popular with them.

Northern soldiers generally carried English-made knives while Confederates relied more on homemade products. Some of these were well made from the best English cast steel, occasionally by former file manufacturers such as Lan & Sherman of Richmond. Other fine knives were made by armories such as that of W. J. McElroy of Macon, Georgia, which was turning out twenty bowie knives a week in 1862. Other Confederate knives were crudely forged by local blacksmiths or cut down from swords. An interesting feature on many Confederate bowie knives is the presence of a knuckle-bow bending in an even curve from the pommel to the base of the grips. This is a unique feature which is almost never found before or after the war.

FIGURE
61

Bowie made by Alexander of Sheffield with the popular "NY" decoration on blade and scabbard. It was owned by a naval officer during the Civil War. The blade is 6 inches long. The mounts are German silver, and the sheath has a red leather veneer.

U. S. NATIONAL MUSEUM

FIGURE
62

American bowie with cast-brass hilt, about 1855–62. The 11⅛-inch blade is unmarked, but it was undoubtedly made by Bown & Tetley of Pittsburgh, who made the bayonet illustrated in figure 75.　　　　　BEN PALMER COLLECTION

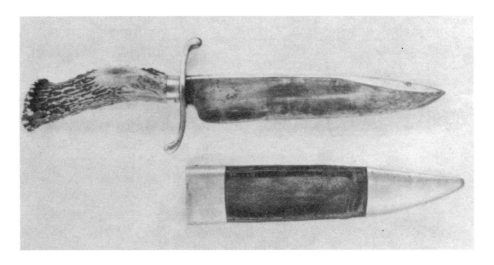

FIGURE
63

American bowie by Hassam, Boston, about 1860–65. The blade is 8⅛ inches long. The guard is iron, but all other mounts are German silver.　　　HERB GLASS COLLECTION

FIGURE
64

A private of the 4th Michigan Infantry in 1861 with his bowie knife thrust through his belt and a Colt revolver on his hip.

NATIONAL ARCHIVES

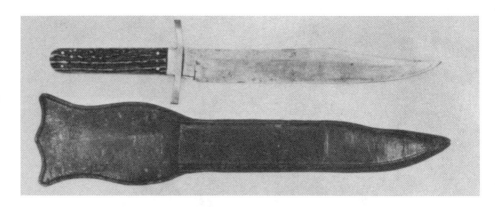

FIGURE
65

Sheffield bowie with 10-inch blade by Joseph Rodgers carried by a Union soldier in the Civil War. The sheath is an American replacement.

WILLIAM SHEMERLUK COLLECTION

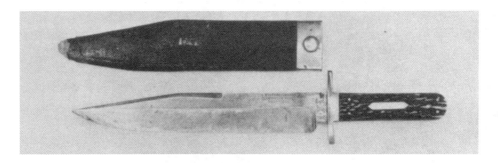

FIGURE
66

Sheffield bowie with 10-inch blade by G. Wostenholm & Son carried by a Union soldier in the Civil War. WILLIAM SHEMERLUK COLLECTION

FIGURE
67

American bowie by C. Roby of West Chelmsford, Mass., 1860–65. The blade is 9¾ inches long. The guard is iron, but the rest of the mounts are brass. The grips are turned wood. WILLIAM SHEMERLUK COLLECTION

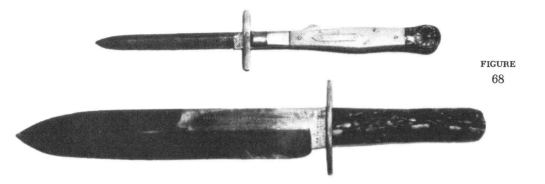

FIGURE
68

John Wilkes Booth's knives. The large knife, by W. F. Jackson of Sheffield, is marked "RIO GRANDE CAMP KNIFE." It was this knife that Booth used to stab Major Rathbone after shooting Lincoln and brandished on the stage of Ford's Theater. The pocket dagger was found on Booth's body when he was killed at Garret's barn.

NATIONAL PARK SERVICE

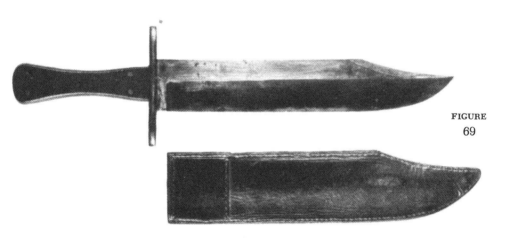

FIGURE
69

Confederate bowie picked up on the Perryville battlefield. The blade is 12⅞ inches long. The grips are wood; the mounts, brass. U. S. NATIONAL MUSEUM

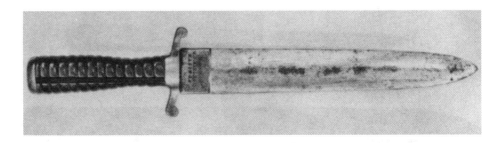

FIGURE
70

Confederate bowie by W. J. McElroy, Macon, Ga., with 12¾-inch blade. The grips are wood; the mounts, brass.   LEON C. JACKSON COLLECTION

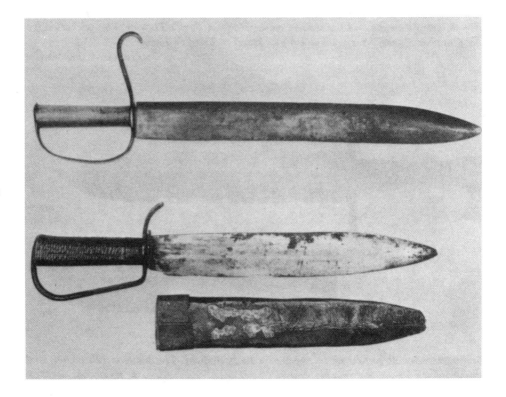

FIGURE
71

Two Confederate bowies with typical knuckle-bows and blades 13¾ and 16 inches long.   WILLIAM SHEMERLUK COLLECTION

FIGURE
72

Confederate bowie with 11¾-inch blade. The grips are wood; the mounts, iron.

LEON C. JACKSON COLLECTION

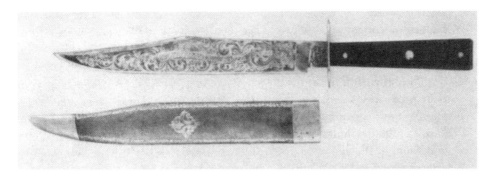

FIGURE
73

Post Civil War bowie made by I. Lingard of Sheffield. The 8¾-inch blade is ornamented with the words "CALIFORNIAN BOWIE KNIFE" and floral scrolls in the late-type gilt etching. The mounts are German silver; the grips, wood; and the scabbard has a yellow-brown leather veneer. HERB GLASS COLLECTION

One final development of the bowie knife during the Civil War was its adaptation as a bayonet. Crude specimens are encountered with wooden grips and double brass loops to fit over the gun barrel. These, according to tradition, were used by Arkansas troops. Bown and Tetley of Pittsburgh produced a better-made type, and so did Boyle, Gamble & MacFee of Richmond. The most widely used knife bayonet of the war, however, was the Dahlgren, which was designed for the so-called Plymouth Navy rifle of 1861. Following the Civil War the idea of combining a bowie knife and a bayonet was dropped until the 1890's, when a small quantity was produced for the Krag rifle for service in the Philippines.

During the twenty-five years from 1840 to 1865, when the popularity of the bowie was at its height, some were used for presentation purposes to distinguished citizens. The practice never became as widespread as the presentation of swords, but occasional specimens are found with such inscriptions. Sometimes a standard model was used with a little extra engraving or plating. At other times knives seem to have been made especially for the purpose just as swords were.

After the Civil War the bowie's popularity declined rapidly. Cowboys and buffalo hunters continued to carry them, but the frontier was swiftly vanishing. The fur trade was almost gone, and civilization was crowding out the big knife. Ironically, this was the period when American cutlers began to make the bowie in quantity, among them Landers, Frary & Clark, Lamson & Goodnow, Collins & Co., the Bridgeport Gun Implement Company and, at the very end, the John Russell Cutlery Company. But these were in reality hunting knives. The fighting bowie had long since disappeared.

The knives of these declining years can easily be distinguished from their predecessors. Aside from the names of manufacturers which are datable and a general shrinking in size, new materials make their appearance. Synthetics imitating bone and ivory appeared about 1870, and celluloid, though developed in 1868, followed later. Hard rubber was popular after the middle 1870's; and finally came plastics for the grips and stainless steel for the blades.

FIGURE
74

Confederate bowie bayonet of the type reputed to have been popular in Arkansas. It was apparently made to fit a Kentucky rifle which had had the end of its octagonal barrel turned round. The blade is 12¼ inches long. The grips are wood, and the mounts, crudely cast brass.   WILLIAM SHEMERLUK COLLECTION

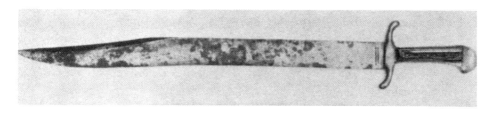

Bowie bayonet made by Bown & Tetley, Pittsburgh, about 1855–62. The blade is 20¼ inches long. The hilt is cast brass.   BEN PALMER COLLECTION

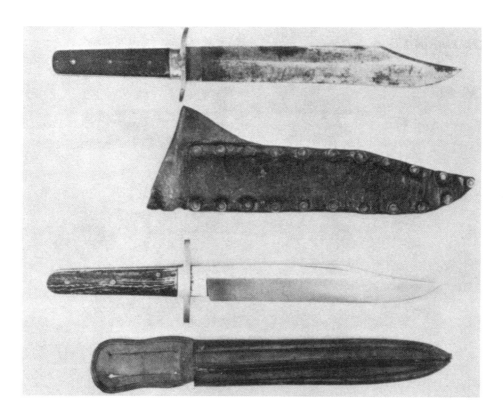

FIGURE
75

FIGURE
76

Two late American bowies. The upper knife with hard rubber grips and an 8½-inch blade was made by the Bridgeport Gun Implement Company (B.G.I.Co.). The brass mounts are nickel-plated. The scabbard is a replacement. The lower knife with an 8-inch blade was made by Landers, Frary & Clark. Its mounts are German silver.
WILLIAM SHEMERLUK COLLECTION

FIGURE
77

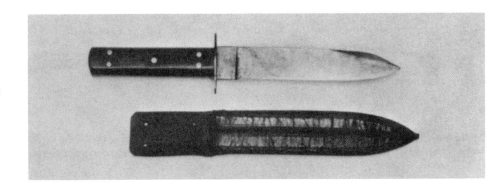

Late knife by Lamson & Goodnow with a 6⅜-inch blade and brass mounts.

HERB GLASS COLLECTION

FIGURE
78

*Late hunting knives by the John Russell Company, 1890–1929. All are marked "*Green
River Works*" in addition to the company name.* JOHN S. DU MONT COLLECTION

But the bowie tradition had not died. For almost half a century it lay dormant. Then, with the advent of World War II and its jungle campaigns, the fighting bowie came back into its own. Service men of all branches bought or made knives of the bowie pattern for their personal use—and they used them both as weapons and tools in the classic tradition. Finally, the Navy and Marine Corps made such a knife an issue arm.

Today bowie knives as fine as any ever forged are being manufactured in small quantities in the United States. W. D. Randall, Jr., of Orlando, Florida, makes several every month on special order. Each is hand-forged from the finest Swedish steel with blades ranging from nine to eleven inches in length. The guards are brass, the grips built up of sole-leather washers and the butt caps made of Duralumin. These modern knives are true heavy-duty fighting and general-utility implements. They are bought by hunters, trappers, prospectors and soldiers who need that type just as their ancestors did a century ago. Through them the bowie tradition lives on.

Alongside the bowie knife stands another very famous knife name of the same era, the Arkansas Toothpick. Students and collectors today try to distinguish between the toothpick and the bowie and use the names for two different kinds of knives. The distinction seems largely modern, however. The men who carried the knives used the terms interchangeably. Arkansas toothpick was a joking nickname coupling the name of the state where the knife was developed and a humorous comment on the huge size of the blade.

As collectors today use the term, however, it applies to a knife with a straight tapering double-edged blade. Actually this is nothing more than the old dagger—still a popular weapon in the early 1800's. The men who used it most often called it a dagger or a dirk-knife.

As a survival of an old established weapon, daggers can be found ranging from the very beginning of the period until its end. Fine silver-mounted specimens were carried by gentlemen and even by high-ranking or wealthy Army officers. Plainer specimens were popular with all classes in the West and have been excavated at several trading-post sites. Rough homemade specimens comparable to the cruder bowies are also found. Gamblers sometimes used a special version with cross grips that could be carried concealed in a special spring-locked scabbard; and to complete the picture, the dagger also was used at times as a presentation weapon.

FIGURE
79

Sheffield bowie by E. S. Stenton presented by J. H. Prioleau of Charleston, S. C., to Capt. Edmund Kirby Smith, 1847–1861. Smith was breveted captain in 1847 for gallantry in the Mexican War. He became a general in the Confederate Army.

WEST POINT MUSEUM

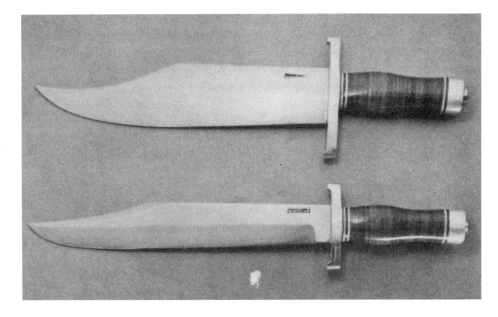

FIGURE
80

Two modern bowies made by W. D. Randall, Jr., of Orlando, Florida.

W. D. RANDALL, JR.

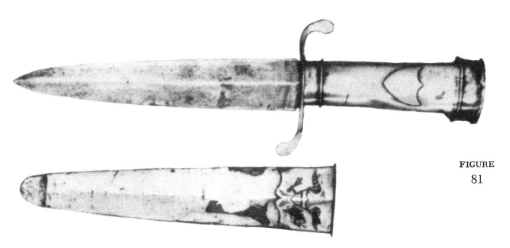

FIGURE
81

American silver-mounted dagger about 1790–1810. The blade is 5½ inches long. The handle is a cylinder of sheet silver filled with a resinous substance.

CHICAGO HISTORICAL SOCIETY

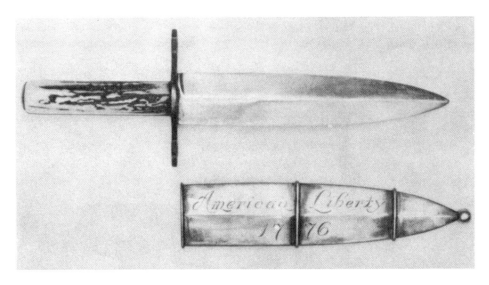

FIGURE
82

American (?) dagger of the early 19th century. The blade is 7⅜ inches long. The guard is iron with pierced decorations, and the scabbard is brass. The inscription is apparently commemorative.

LEON C. JACKSON COLLECTION

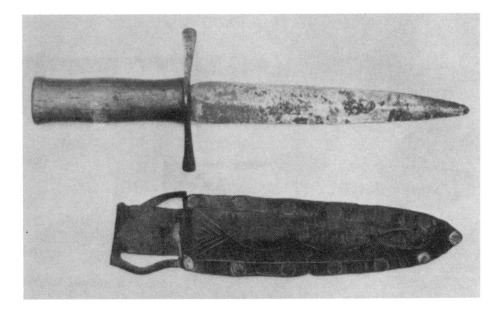

FIGURE
83

Crudely-made American dagger of the middle 19th century, said to have been found in the Southwest. The 8½-inch blade is made from a file. The guard is iron, and the sheath is fastened with copper rivets.   WILLIAM SHEMERLUK COLLECTION

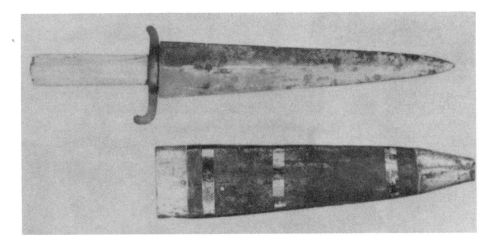

FIGURE
84

American dagger of the mid-19th century. The heavy blade is 12¾ inches long. The grips are bone, and the guard has apparently been put on upside down. The scabbard is made of wood with brass mounts.   BEN PALMER COLLECTION

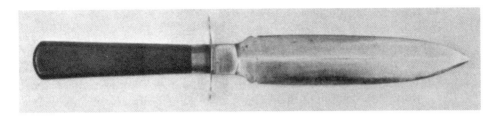

FIGURE
85

American dagger about 1860–80. The 8-inch blade is stamped "H. WILKINSON/HART-FORD CT." The guard is German silver; the ferrule is brass; and the grips are wood.

WILLIAM SHEMERLUK COLLECTION

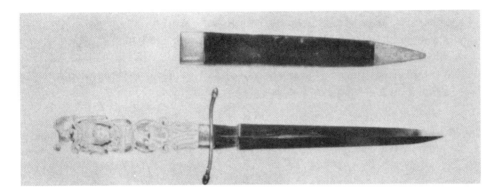

FIGURE
86

Presentation dagger given by the citizens of Boston to Francis E. Brownell (see frontis-piece) during the Civil War. The blade is 7⅞ inches long and undecorated. The grips are carved ivory, and the mountings are silver. The body of the scabbard is velvet.

U. S. NATIONAL MUSEUM

One special form of the dagger did develop during this period, how-ever, which is not encountered among the colonial daggers. This was the folding or pocket dagger. These ranged in size from tiny specimens with four- or five-inch blades to great long affairs with blades up to sixteen and three-eighths inches in length. Most of these folding daggers were designed to be carried in the pocket, but others had special sheaths. Some of these latter types could be used either open or closed, depending on the length of blade the owner felt he needed for any given job.

Although the bowie knife and/or the Arkansas toothpick were cer-tainly the most widely known knives of their era and achieved the greatest historical fame, they were by no means the only forms of sheath knives carried in the American West. The trappers and traders, the mountain men, who explored the Rockies and braved the Sioux and Blackfoot in search of beaver, flourished well before James Bowie had his knife made. These men carried knives similar to those of the eighteenth-century riflemen, typical butcher knives or knives shaped from files and hilted with antler. Even after the advent of the bowie, these men tended to hold to their old patterns.

Most of the mountain men's early store-bought knives came from England, but after 1834 they got one all their own. In that year John Russell began the manufacture of butcher and carving knives on the Green River at Greenfield, Massachusetts. Many of these knives were shipped west, most often to Pierre Chouteau, Jr., & Co. From the trading posts of this famous fur company the knives were purchased by the hunters, trappers and Indians. An idea of the quantity of Russell's knives which were dispersed throughout the upper Missouri River region can be had from the fact that the average number of knives shipped west each year from 1840 to 1860 was five thousand dozen. These sold wholesale at $1.50 to $3.50 a dozen and retailed at the fur posts for fifty cents to $1.50 each.

FIGURE
87

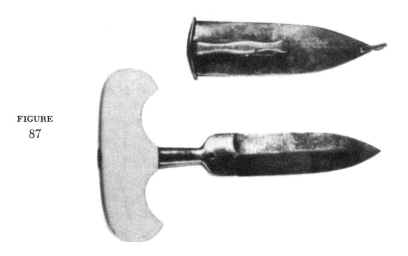

*Push dagger of the type popular with gamblers in the West, 1848–60. The 4-inch blade is marked "*WILLS & FINK*/S. F. *CAL*." The grips are ivory. The iron scabbard is designed to hang upside down while the blade is retained by a spring.*
U. S. NATIONAL MUSEUM

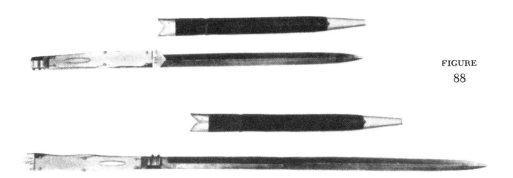

FIGURE
88

Sheffield folding dirk closed and fully extended. When open, the blade is 16⅜ inches long; when closed, 10⅛ inches. Note the American eagle stamped on the German silver mounts of the handle. The grips are ivory. The scabbard is red leather.

WILLIAM SHEMERLUK COLLECTION

The new knives found favor immediately, and the term "Green River" became a part of the trapper's vocabulary. Frederick Ruxton, in 1848, wrote of the mountain men in his *Life in the Far West*: "For, as may be imagined, a thrust from the keen scalp-knife by the nervous arm of a mountaineer was no baby blow and seldom failed to strike home—up to the 'Green River' on the blade." In this Ruxton referred to the fact that Russell's knives were stamped "J. Russell & Co./Green River Works" on the blade near the hilt. Any knife thrust in "up to the 'Green River'" would have done a thorough job. "Give it to 'em up to the Green River!" became a recognized battle cry. At the same time the term "Green River" or "up to Green River" also became synonymous for anything well done or well made. Thus anything done "up to Green River" was first rate.

The knives which created this impact on the life and speech of the mountain men were not prepossessing in appearance. They were well made and boasted fine blades, but otherwise they were simple butcher and carving knives, the same as might have been found in any New England kitchen. Two of the most popular models sent west, according to company records, were known as "Butcher Knife No. 15," which had a six-inch blade, and "Carving Knife No. 1586," which had an eight-inch blade. Butcher's skinning knives used in the early West are also found quite frequently. The early knives were stamped "J. Russell & Co./Green River Works" in two lines. Later a diamond-shaped stamp was placed below it. Some time before 1890 the company changed from stamped to etched marks, and finally the commemorative date 1834 was added to some knives.

One change took place almost universally on the knives sent west. The new owner changed the edge of his purchase. Like most cutlers, J. Russell & Co. sharpened their knives evenly, beveling both sides of the blade. The purchasers who wanted to use the knives for skinning ground off the old edge and put the bevel all on one side. This new edge let them skin with less danger of piercing the hide and lowering its value. As a word of caution, it should be noted that many of the Green River knives actually used in the West have been sharpened so many times that their shape is often entirely different from what it was when it left the factory.

When Russell started in business, the Sheffield cutlers did everything they could to interfere. They even dumped quantities of knives on the American market at prices well below cost. Finally, however, they had to admit that the Russell Company was going to stay in business. Then they paid him the ultimate compliment of producing somewhat similar knives also bearing the name "Green River." "Green River" knives made in England can still be purchased today.

FIGURE
89

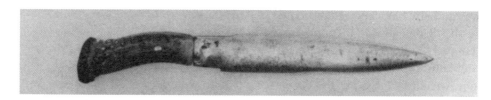

Rifle knife made from a half-round file, early 19th century. The blade is 7¼ inches long. When found, the knife was still in its sheath fastened to the strap of a rifle bag.

ROBERT ALBRECHT COLLECTION

FIGURE
90

Unusually fine rifle knife, about 1830–40. The blade is 5¼ inches long, and the handle is decorated with German silver and mother-of-pearl inlays to match the rifle it was designed to accompany.   WILLIAM SHEMERLUK COLLECTION

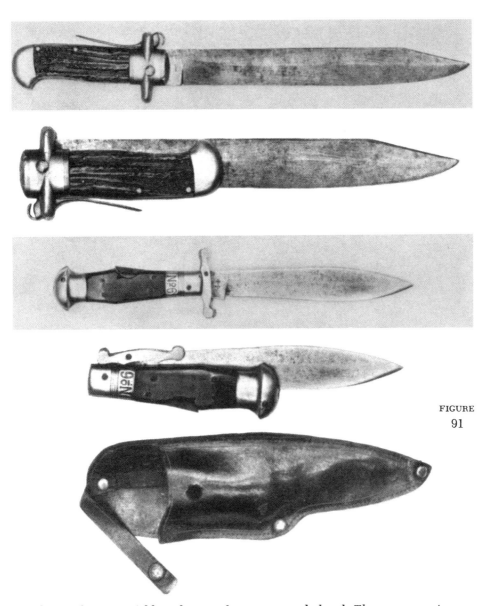

FIGURE
91

Two late 19th-century folding daggers shown open and closed. The upper specimen is German. The lower knife, which retains its scabbard, is English. When open, the blades are 9⅝ and 6⅛ inches respectively. Both are mounted in German silver. The German knife has antler handles; the English has horn.

LEON C. JACKSON COLLECTION

FIGURE
92

Group of J. Russell "Green River" knives. The top three bear the early stamped mark. The bottom four are skinning knives and have the later etched marks.

JOHN S. DU MONT COLLECTION

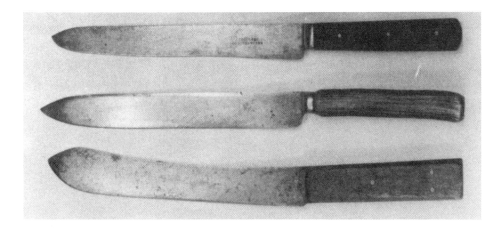

FIGURE
93

Typical Russell "Green River" butcher knives. The upper specimen is the earliest. All are representative of those shipped West. JOHN S. DU MONT COLLECTION

FIGURE
94

Sheffield skinning knife by I. Wilson, about 1890, with "Green River" stamped on the blade. A group of these knives was found recently in an Alaskan trading post, still packed in a cask of moose tallow. AUTHOR'S COLLECTION

FIGURE
95

*Sheffield knife by George Butler & Co., which also is imitatively marked "*GREEN RIVER KNIFE.*" This pattern is still being manufactured.*

JOHN S. DU MONT COLLECTION

These were the most popular knives in the winning of the West: the colorful bowie and Arkansas toothpick in their many variations; the dagger; and the more prosaic but equally efficient Green River knife. With these were a host of other knives, the handmade types previously mentioned and other manufactured varieties in the hands of both civilians and soldiers, to be described in following chapters. None, however, will ever attain the place in American legend held by the bowie.

CHAPTER IV

ARMY KNIVES

FIGURE
96

Hicks knife with half knuckle-bow and sheath.   COL. B. R. LEWIS COLLECTION

A SOLDIER in the field is a man on his own. Behind the lines there are dozens of noncombatants to take care of his needs. As he nears the fighting area these helpers gradually melt away until in the final phase there are only other fighting men. Now the soldier prepares his own food, constructs his own shelter, makes emergency repairs to his own equipment and defends his own life. In all these activities he gratefully accepts the services of a good knife.

Any man who has been in a combat area knows how highly a soldier prizes his knife. It is evident in the way he handles it and in the way he takes care of it. And especially in the lengths to which he will go to obtain one that meets his personal requirements. In the Pacific during World War II fighting men set tremendous store by their knives. Despite the fact that they were issued adequate knives, they often encountered others they liked better in the hands of sailors or rear-echelon soldiers. Then nothing would stand in their way until they got it. Money, food, trophies, anything—even

71

whisky, that most precious of all commodities to a soldier in the Pacific theater, would be offered until the sale was made.

This close relationship between a soldier and his knife has prevailed throughout recorded history. It has been obvious to every military man who ever participated in a campaign. Yet, strangely enough, the idea of issuing a knife to all combat troops is relatively recent. Special units have been equipped with knives at government expense from the very beginning, but the average soldier was expected to provide his own.

Such privately purchased knives reflected the individual soldier's personal preferences, and consequently a great variety were used. Most soldiers carried a pocketknife of some sort. In the early years it was probably a jack-knife such as those required by some states during the Revolution. Later the more versatile pocketknives of the middle 1800's became commoner. The bowie knife was also a great favorite during the Mexican War and the opening years of the Civil War. It fell from favor during the last years of that conflict but again became very popular with the Indian fighting armies in the West during the 1870's and '80's. These last soldiers, especially the cavalry, also often carried simple butcher knives of the Green River types in handmade leather sheaths on their belts. Some daggers were carried, too, but in much smaller numbers. In fact, it would be hard to find any form of knife currently available that was not represented by at least one or two specimens somewhere in the army.

The special troops for whom the government provided knives prior to 1861 were primarily riflemen. Up to 1855 the Regular Infantry were armed with smooth-bored muskets. From time to time, however, specially selected units were formed and armed with rifles. Sometimes they were organized in separate regiments and sometimes scattered in individual companies in Regular Infantry regiments or in legions. Generally speaking, riflemen appeared in numbers during crises and disappeared in periods of retrenchment. There were riflemen also in state militia units, and under the famous Militia Act of 1808, these troops too were equipped by the federal government.

The knives which these early riflemen carried closely resembled those of the Revolutionary riflemen. Official records refer to them variously as "butcher," "scalping," or "hunting" knives. There are no existing descriptions of these knives, no contracts have survived and no existing specimen has even been identified. From casual references in the documents, however, it is known that they had plain wooden handles, that the blades were eight to ten inches long and from one inch to an inch and a half wide and that they were normally issued with sheaths and waist belts. Thus, taking into consideration the general practices of the period, it would seem safe to assume that these rifleman's knives were indeed butcher knives as we understand the term today.

The knives of later riflemen, fortunately, are better known. In the late 1830's or early 1840's Andrew G. Hicks, a widely traveled cutler and tool-maker of Cleveland, Ohio, made a large number of military knives. No specific government contract with Hicks has survived, but in the letter books of the "Allegany Arsenal" there are frequent references to Hicks, knives and purchases. The general implication is that the arsenal, which handled procurement of supplies for the region west of the Alleghenies, purchased these knives from Hicks to supply the demands of various state governments for their militia.

Hicks's knives are well made, have a military appearance and are quite rare today. Collectors set great store by them. The grips are walnut strongly bound with brass strips which are secured by fourteen separate screws! The guard is likewise brass, and the stout blade is ten inches long and one and a half inches wide. The maker's mark, stamped in the wood of the grips, is "A. G. HICKS/MAKER/CLEV'D O." A study of the existing specimens of Hicks's knives reveals that there were several minor variations. The point of the blade is sometimes clipped, sometimes almost a spear. Some of the handles have a convex iron pommel cap held by two large iron screws, while others have a flat brass cap which is extended and bent to form a partial knuckle-bow. Only one scabbard has thus far been located. It is made of black leather with a brass tip, throat and frog stud and is decidedly military in appearance.

FIGURE
97

Variant of the Hicks knife with convex iron butt cap and slightly different blade.
LEON C. JACKSON COLLECTION

In 1848 the Ordnance Department contracted for the first rifleman's knife made to a specific government pattern. On March 8 of that year they signed a contract with James T. Ames of the Ames Manufacturing Company, Cabotville, Massachusetts, for "1000 knives for the Regiment of Mounted Riflemen . . . the heaviest & largest of the Lot presented by Mr. Ames." The price agreed upon was four dollars per knife, and the entire lot was delivered May 5, 1849.

The Ames knife was a formidable weapon, both longer and heavier than those made by Hicks. The blade was eleven and three quarter inches long and one and five eighths inches wide. It had a spear point and a short false edge. The guard was brass, and the handle had walnut scales pierced at the pommel for a lanyard or thong. The blade was stamped "AMES MFG CO./CABOTVILLE/1849" on the obverse ricasso and "U.S." and "WD" (the inspector's initials) on the reverse side. The guard also bore two sets of inspector's initials, "W.D." and "J.W.R." The scabbard was of black leather with brass tip and throat. It had a stud for attachment to a frog. All in all, it was a highly finished and well-designed knife.

The Regiment of Mounted Riflemen, for whom these knives were intended, had been organized in 1846 at Fort McHenry in Baltimore. It served with honor during the Mexican War and had the distinction of being the first Regular Army unit to be equipped with Colt revolvers—the famous Walker Colts. In 1861 it became the 3rd Cavalry Regiment. Today it is the 3rd Armored Cavalry Regiment and bears the proud name "The Brave Rifles."

After the Ames contract there was a lapse of thirty-one years before another official Army knife was issued. Then the Springfield Armory began production of the model 1880 hunting knife. Almost all armory and Ordnance Board records relating to this knife are now lost, and so little is known about the background of its design or its intended use. There is one Board report that the knife had been tested by a group of officers who thought it a fine knife but felt that the blade was a little too brittle even "for the ordinary purposes for which it was intended." What these purposes were is never indicated, but the Board recommended that such knives with better steel blades be issued to both cavalry and infantry. Probably it was supposed to be an all-purpose camp knife, designed particularly for the Army in the West. Its name seems to imply such a purpose. It certainly is not a good fighting knife, and it seems to be too light for any really heavy

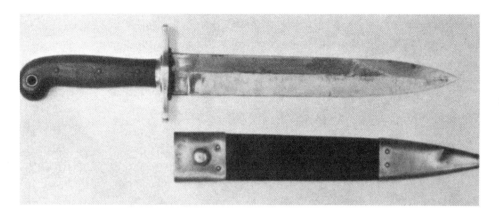

Ames rifleman's knife, 1849.

WILLIAM SHEMERLUK COLLECTION

FIGURE
98

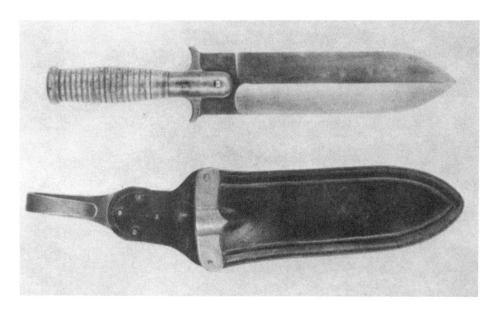

U. S. Army hunting knife, model 1880.

AUTHOR'S COLLECTION

FIGURE
99

Group of soldiers photographed in the early 1890's. Note that one wears the 1880 hunting knife on the right side of the belt and two wear it on the left.

FIGURE
100

service. The blade is eight and a half inches long with a single edge and a spear point. The guard is brass and is slotted to receive the base of the blade. The grips are turned wood with a light natural finish. Usually the guard is stamped with a serial number on the obverse side and "U.S./ SPRINGFIELD" on the reverse. The scabbards were made primarily at Rock Island and Watervliet Arsenals. They are heavy black sole leather with a brass plate on the outside of the throat and an iron plate on the inside. The arsenal's name is frequently stamped on the inside of the leather flap. On some there is also a wide brass belt hook which usually bears the name of the arsenal stamped on its back. On others there is a leather belt loop.

In 1887 another similar knife was adopted by the Army, this time for its hospital corpsmen. Theoretically they were to use it for cutting splints, shaping or removing casts, slitting clothing and other similar duties. The corpsman's knife was bigger than the hunting knife but still seems too light for heavy duty. Probably because of this fact surviving records indicate that only 650 of these knives were manufactured in 1888 and 1889.

The Hospital Corps knife differed only slightly from the hunting knife. It had a longer blade (twelve and one-eighth inches) which bore an etched panel with the legend "HOSPITAL CORPS/U. S. ARMY" in large letters. The brass guard was nickel plated and was also slightly larger and more functional. In addition there was a metal pommel cap. The scabbard differed only in length. Once again, some had a leather belt loop and some a brass hook.

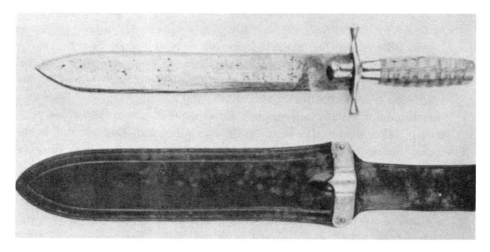

FIGURE
101

Hospital Corps knife, model 1887.   U. S. NATIONAL MUSEUM

About this time a very similar knife was made by Collins & Co. of Hartford, Connecticut, for the use of some state troops. It had dark wood grips, brass mounts, a slightly different guard and bore the Collins mark with no etched panel, but otherwise it was almost identical. The scabbard was different in that it had a brass tip and was fitted with a frog. These Collins knives were undoubtedly intended for fighting or other all-around uses, not for medical corpsmen. The specimen illustrated herewith is stamped "1 N.Y.F." on the grips. This might refer to a unit name, such as the New York Fusiliers or Fencibles, but the State Adjutant General has been unable to confirm any such designation. It is also marked "No. 26" on the scabbard.

FIGURE
102

Collins knife similar to the Hospital Corps knife. It is stamped "INYF" on the grips, and "No 26" is scratched on the scabbard.   COL. B. R. LEWIS COLLECTION

In 1898 came the Spanish-American War followed closely by the Philippine Insurrection. The jungle campaigns of these struggles were the first in which American soldiers had participated, and they pointed to the need for a heavy knife that could be used for both fighting and clearing a path through the thick undergrowth. Experimentation was begun, first with the idea of combining the heavy knife with a bayonet. This resulted in the famous bowie bayonet for the Krag rifle, a bolo bayonet, a new Hospital Corps knife, and finally the bolo itself.

Both the bowie and bolo bayonets were colorful weapons, and both are scarce items today. The bowie bayonet had a thin slightly curved blade nine and one-eighth inches long with a clipped point. Interestingly, it was

FIGURE
103

The Krag bowie and bolo bayonets.   U. S. NATIONAL MUSEUM

double-choiled, and while the back was sharpened for two and a half inches near the hilt, the arca of the usual false edge was swaged only. They were marked on the obverse side with the letters "US" and on the reverse with the date, usually 1900. The scabbard was blued steel with a steel belt loop. Because the blade was thin it did not make the rifle muzzle-heavy when attached. At the same time, however, it was sturdy enough for most tasks, if not for cutting heavy brush.

The bolo bayonet, on the other hand, was a heavy brush-cutting tool, and it was definitely awkward when attached to the rifle. It had a blued blade ten and one-quarter inches long, two and one-eighth inches wide and three-eighths of an inch thick. There was a short false edge, bevelled equally on both sides, but most of the bevel of the regular edge was on the obverse side only.

The new Hospital Corps knife, developed in 1904, was also, in reality, a bolo. It had a wide curved blade, twelve inches long, with a rounded point, and the bevel of the edge all on the obverse side. The guard was brass, and the wooden grips had sharply defined finger notches. The scabbard was russet leather with a brass throat and either a pivoted blued steel belt loop or a simple leather one. All of these bolos were stamped on the obverse

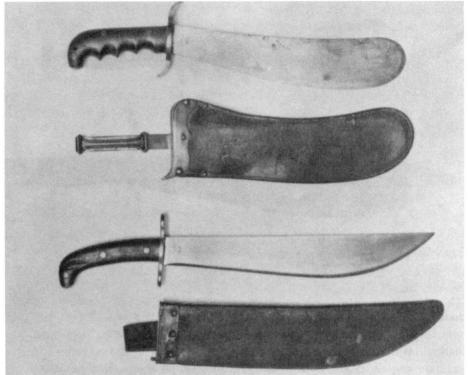

FIGURE
104

The model 1904 Hospital Corps knife (above) and the model 1909 bolo.

side of the blade with the letters "U.S." and a serial number and on the reverse side with the date of manufacture and sometimes also the initials of the Armory separated by a flaming bomb. Production began late in 1904 and continued intermittently through 1913, with a total output of 6,502 listed.

Because this new Hospital Corps knife was an excellent tool, it may well have been used by other troops as a bolo. As a weapon, however, it had a major drawback in its lack of a point. This fault was corrected in the official bolos of the period which were issued generally to line troops.

In all, the United States authorized four specific models of the bolo, the 1909, 1910, 1917, and 1917CT. The 1909 bolo had a heavy blade thirteen and seven-eighths inches long which increased in both width and thickness towards the point to throw the balanced forward for more effective chopping. Again, all the edge bevel was on the obverse side. The guard was iron, pierced for a stud on the scabbard throat. The grips were wood, and resembled those on the 1904 hospital knife except that they lacked finger notches. The scabbard was heavy sole leather with a brass throat and a simple leather belt loop. All of these bolos were made at the Springfield Armory, and they were marked on the obverse side with "U.S." above a serial number and on the reverse with "SA," a flaming bomb and the date of manufacture. Production began in 1909 and continued at least through 1912 and possibly into 1915; the production figures are not clear.

The model 1910 bolo utilized the same blade shape and general hilt conformation as the earlier bolo bayonet. The guard differed in being made of lighter stock, in not being pierced for the gun barrel and in having a thumb-spring catch to secure it in its scabbard. The pommel was shorter and differed otherwise in not being fitted with a groove and latch for the bayonet stud. It was a short compact weapon with a heavy blued single-edged blade ten and one-quarter inches long and two and one-eight inches wide. There was a short false edge. The grips were roughly finished walnut, and the pommel and guard were blued steel. The blade was stamped with "U.S." and serial number on the obverse side and "S.A." (Springfield Armory), date and flaming bomb on the reverse. There were at least two types of scabbard, one with a wooden lining covered with webbing reinforced at the tip with heavy leather and one made of stamped sheet iron. Both had a brass wire hook for attachment to the belt. Most scabbards bore a date, armory mark and inspector's initials on the reverse side.

It was not a pretty weapon, but it was efficient. The wide heavy blade with its balance well forward made it an excellent chopping tool or weapon. The 1918 *Handbook of Ordnance Data* described it as a "heavy brush knife, useful for clearing brush, sharpening pegs, or valuable for personal combat in extreme cases."

Both the models 1917 and 1917CT were almost identical to the 1910. In the 1917 the only change was the removal of the scabbard catch. In the 1917CT the pommel was made integral with the tang and the guard was welded. In the 1917 the guard was slipped over the tang, and the pommel was brazed on. Neither the 1917 nor the 1917CT was made at Springfield.

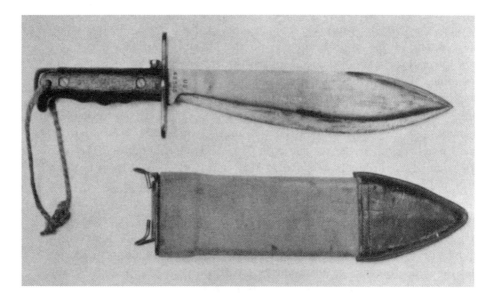

FIGURE
105

The model 1910 bolo. The hole and thong were added by the Marine who used this bolo during World War II. LT. COL. F. B. NIHART COLLECTION

FIGURE
106

The model 1917 bolo with alternate scabbard. Note that the scabbard catch has been removed from the hilt but that the hole remains in the guard. WEST POINT MUSEUM

FIGURE
107

The model 1917 trench knife.   WEST POINT MUSEUM

Both were manufactured under contract, principally by Fayette R. Plumb, the American Cutlery Company and the Bartlett Edge Tool Company.

Once it had been adopted, the bolo remained in use at least until the close of World War II. In the years between the two World Wars, practically the only demand for the heavy knife came from the Philippines. In 1923 and again in 1927 the question of dropping it as a standard ordnance item was raised, but since there were stocks on hand it was decided to retain the model 1917 bolo as an issue item until the stock had been exhausted and then purchase locally whatever bolos were needed in the Philippines. When World War II broke out, however, many of the older Navy ships still carried the model 1910 and 1917 bolos among their landing stores. The idea of a bolo bayonet also recurred. In 1921 several were manufactured and tested in the Infantry School at Fort Benning, but they were never adopted.

The bolo had been primarily a tool and only secondarily a weapon. In 1917 the United States began production of another knife that was a weapon only—the trench knife. World War I had been characterized by trench warfare. Whole armies lay within sight of each other, dug into semi-permanent earth fortifications. Actions were characterized by patrol clashes and by full-scale assaults "over the top" culminating in hand-to-hand encounters. Frequently these occurred within the confined area of a trench where the rifle and bayonet were unwieldy. Sometimes on raids silence was desired. For these situations a knife was considered the ideal weapon, and the Ordnance Department set out to produce one. The problem was discussed with a number of manufacturers, and in the end, the knife designed by Henry Disston & Sons of Philadelphia was selected.

This new knife, known as the model 1917 trench knife, was strictly a stabbing weapon. Its narrow nine-inch blade was triangular in cross section and tapered evenly to a point. This form of blade had been chosen because of the ease with which it would pierce clothing and even leather. The grips were made of a single piece of wood. The knuckle-bow was stamped from a sheet of iron with pyramidal knobs down the center of the bow so that a blow delivered with the fist would have a devastating effect. The sheath was cylindrical, with iron throat and tip, and all metal parts of both knife and sheath were blued. The maker's initials, the letters "U.S." and the date were usually stamped on the blade side of the quillon. In 1918 the knuckle-bow was altered slightly, and triangular flanges on both sides of the knuckle-bow replaced the pyramidal knobs in the center. This new knife was designated the model 1918. Both knives were made under contract by Landers, Frary & Clark, who produced 113,000, and the Oneida Community Ltd. of Oneida, New York, who made ten thousand.

Combat troops did not like either the 1917 or 1918 trench knives. They were too specialized, allowing only two strokes in combat, and they were of no earthly use as a tool for opening cans, carving wood or any of the

FIGURE 108

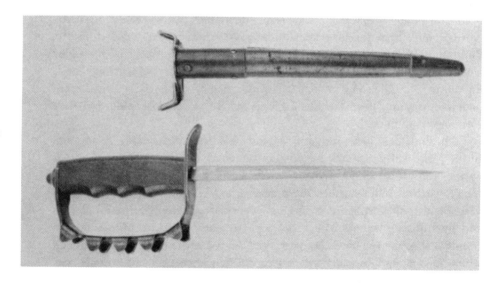

The model 1918 trench knife and scabbard. Both the models 1917 and 1918 trench knives used the same scabbard.   WEST POINT MUSEUM

other tasks a soldier's knife should perform. On June 1, 1918, the American Expeditionary Forces made an exhaustive test of the various trench knives used by the Allied Armies to rate their suitability on the following points:

(a) Serviceability—ability to carry in hand and function other arms
(b) Quickness in action
(c) If the soldier were knocked unconscious, would knife drop from hand?
(d) Suitability to carry in hand when crawling
(e) Probability of being knocked out of hand
(f) Weight, length, shape of blade
(g) Shape of handle

As a result of these tests, the A.E.F. and the Ordnance Department designed an entirely new knife, the Mark I, which supposedly combined the best points of all the knives used by the foreign armies. It had a flat double-edged blade six and three-quarter inches long and one inch wide that could be used for cutting as well as thrusting. The hilt was cast bronze with individual finger loops. The scabbard was iron, either with flanges or with a brass wire loop on the back through which the belt could be passed. Both the scabbard and blade were blued, and sometimes the hilts were blackened also. The obverse side of the grips bore the legend "U S 1918/ L F & C—1918." Originally the government placed orders for 1,232,780 of these knives with several manufacturers, but the Armistice caused all to be canceled except for one lot of 119,424 made by Landers, Frary & Clark.

Immediately after this new knife had been adopted and before Landers, Frary & Clark could get into production, a small quantity of Mark I knives were purchased for the United States from French manufacturers. These differed from the standard American-made knife in having only the legend "U.S.—1918" on the grips and the maker's mark stamped on the blade. The points of the knuckle loops also were slightly different.

After the close of World War I there was no need for a fighting knife for a period of more than twenty years. In 1922 both the models 1917 and 1918 were declared obsolete and were disposed of, but an Infantry Board recommended the retention of the Mark I, which was not declared obsolete until January, 1945.

As World War II approached, the United States began experimenting with air-borne troops who could be parachuted to strategic spots. These paratroopers, as they came to be called, needed a knife that could be used to cut themselves free from their parachutes. It had to be a knife that could

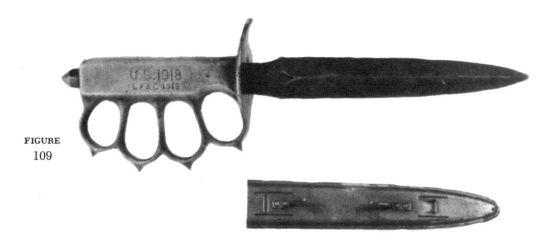

FIGURE
109

The Mark I trench knife and scabbard (reverse side) manufactured by Landers, Frary & Clark.   WEST POINT MUSEUM

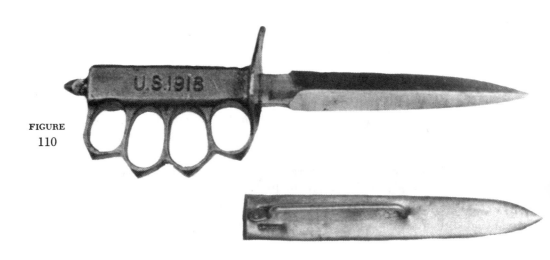

FIGURE
110

Mark I trench knife and scabbard (reverse side) made in France.
                              WAR MEMORIAL MUSEUM OF VIRGINIA

be drawn and used easily with one hand. The Mark I was too clumsy, so a new knife was designed, and in 1940 the first fifty experimental models were ordered from the Schrade Cutlery Company of Walden, New York. These were folding knives with spring-activated blades that opened by pressing a button on the side. They were seven and three-quarter inches long when open, four and one-half inches long when closed, and weighed only four ounces. The handles were imitation antler. This knife was officially adopted in December, 1940, and designated the pocketknife Mark 2. It was superseded by the Mark 3 in 1943, but in response to a special request from the Pacific Theater a final lot of 1,020 was ordered from Schrade in 1944.

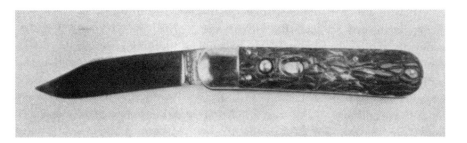

FIGURE
111

Mark 2 paratrooper's knife. The staple for a lanyard is missing from this specimen.
WEST POINT MUSEUM

On December 7, 1941, World War II came to the United States, and within a few weeks there arose a demand for fighting knives. The first request to reach the Chief of Ordnance came from the Military Liaison Officer in Bandung, Indonesia. At that time the only fighting knife in stock was the Mark I. At first it was proposed to restandardize that model, but in the end the Infantry Board decided against it for two reasons: It had a bronze hilt, and bronze was a critical strategic material; they felt that a stronger and more versatile knife could be designed. After studying several designs they selected one and designated it the Mark 3. The official *Catalog of Standard Ordnance Items* has this to say about it:

> The Trench Knife M3 has been developed to fill the need in modern warfare for hand-to-hand fighting. While designated for issue to soldiers not armed with the bayonet, it was especially designed for such shock units as parachute troops and rangers.

The shaped and corrugated handle is of leather washers under compression. One cutting edge runs the full length of the blade; the other edge of the blade is ground to a cutting edge 2¾ inches from the point, then tapers to a thicker section for rigidity and strength.

The knife weighs 9 ounces and measures 11.7 inches over-all, the blade is 6.7 inches long.

Production of the Mark 3 began in 1943. The Pal Blade & Tool Company and the Utica Cutlery Company were scheduled to produce 98,000 at the rate of 20,000 a month. Later, contracts were made with the Camillus Cutlery Co., Imperial Knife Co., Kinfolks Inc. and W. R. Case & Sons. In all, a total of 2,590,247 M3 knives were manufactured before production ceased in August, 1944.

There were two minor changes in the knife itself and two scabbards during its history. At first the knives were marked on the blade, but this made the blades apt to break at the point of stamping, and so the marks were shifted to the guard. Also, soldiers in the Pacific complained that the leather grips became moldy and disintegrated, so a fungicide treatment was developed to prevent mold and mildew. The first scabbard, known as the M6, was all leather, but it was felt that it did not offer sufficient protection. Thus, the M8, a plastic scabbard, was adopted. This had a belt loop that would only fit the pistol belt, and so a modification, the M8A1, was adopted to make it more universally usable.

All of the scabbards were made to be worn on the belt, but many soldiers preferred to carry the knife strapped to their right boot, and they adapted the scabbard for that purpose. There were so many other items of equipment already on the belt that it was cumbersome. Also, with the knife on the boot, it was always available even when the belt had been removed, thus lessening the chance of being surprised without a weapon.

The M3 trench knife was originally designed for troops who were not armed with rifles and who therefore did not have bayonets. As the war progressed, these troops began increasingly to be armed with the carbine, and in July, 1944, the M3 was modified to serve as a bayonet for the carbine and designated the M4 bayonet-knife. Later, since there was still trouble with the leather grips, a plastic handle was adopted.

While the trench knives M3 and M4 were being adopted there was also some experimentation with the British Sykes-Fairbirn commando-type knife or stiletto. This was a slender double-edged knife with a one-piece cast hilt. It was a good stabbing weapon, but brittle and too light for heavy

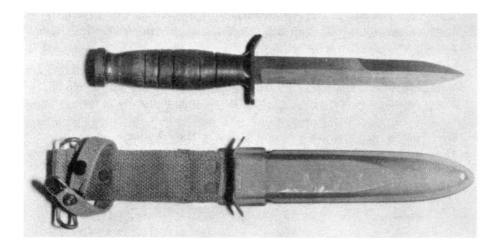

Mark 3 trench knife with Mark 8A1 scabbard. WAR MEMORIAL MUSEUM OF VIRGINIA

FIGURE
112

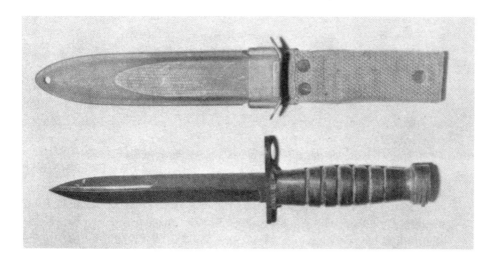

Mark 4 bayonet-knife with scabbard M8. WAR MEMORIAL MUSEUM OF VIRGINIA

FIGURE
113

duty. Nevertheless, during the winter of 1942–43 tests were made by the Tank Destroyer Board, and orders were placed with W. R. Case & Sons Cutlery Company for 3,420 of these knives. They were all delivered by November, 1943, equipped with leather sheaths, and designated Commando Knives Type V-42. It is not known whether any saw actual service. Many American soldiers did use similar commando knives of British manufacture, however, which they purchased personally while stationed in England before embarking for North Africa or the Continent. And the U. S. Marine Corps adopted the pattern for a short period early in the war, as described in the next chapter.

FIGURE

114

British Commando stiletto of the type purchased by many American soldiers.
WEST POINT MUSEUM

There was also one other official fighting knife of World War II, which resembled none of the others. It was characterized primarily by its cast-brass hilt, which had a knuckle-bow with lugs on the outside so that it could be used as a set of brass knuckles. The blade was nine and three-eighths inches long with a clipped point, and the finish throughout was somewhat rough. The scabbard was black leather with a simple belt loop and no metal mounts. Most specimens seem to have been unmarked, but the one illustrated has the letters "US" stamped on the obverse side of the grips. Except for the narrow grips, which did not afford a good hold, it was an excellent fighting and heavy-duty knife.

The standard references in the Office of the Chief of Ordnance offer no evidence that this knife ever existed as an official weapon. The specimens themselves are in existence, however, and at least one veteran claimed to know what they were. According to his statement, they were designed by the 1st Army Ranger Battalion early in 1942 and were carried by that unit. He thought that they might also have been issued to the 2nd Ranger Battalion, but he could not vouch for it from personal knowledge. This, of course, is not positive proof, since there is no official documentation, but many knives were designed and purchased in small quantities for such units without being listed among official Ordnance stores.

FIGURE
115

Special knife of the 1st Ranger Battalion.   WILLIAM SHEMERLUK COLLECTION

Many soldiers were not issued knives of any kind, either because they were not combat troops or because they were armed with rifle and bayonet or for some other similar reason. Ordnance believed that such men did not need a knife, but many of the individual soldiers felt differently. Thus, privately purchased knives again became fairly common in the Army. Among them were the British stiletto, which was quite common among American troops in Europe, knives of every imaginable design fabricated by those enlisted men with access to a machine shop and knives purchased from manufacturers and dealers in the United States. Some of the knives in this last category were standard hunting knives; some were copies of the bowie and some were newly designed fighting and all-purpose knives. Among these new specially designed knives, two of the best were manufactured by W. D. Randall, Jr., of Orlando, Florida, and they had wide popularity in the armed forces both in the war and during the Korean conflict. These were known as the "Model 1, All-purpose Fighting Knife" and the "Model 2, Fighting Stiletto." Both were made with six-, seven- or eight-inch blades, brass cross guards, grips built up of leather washers and butt caps of Duralumin. The sheaths were made of russet saddle leather with a belt loop on the outside of which was sewed a strap to snap around the handle. Each sheath also had a pocket for a hone. Judging from the soldier letters in Randall's files, both of these knives saw considerable combat duty in all theaters of World War II and again in Korea.

FIGURE
116

Model 1 fighting knife (below) and model 2 fighting stiletto (above) manufactured by W. D. Randall, Jr., from World War II to the present.   W. D. RANDALL, JR.

One final knife should also be mentioned among those used by American soldiers during the war, and that is the O.S.S. escape knife. The Office of Strategic Services combined both Army and Navy personnel, and both Army and Navy knives were used. The Navy knife will be discussed later. The one most often included in O.S.S. escape kits, however, was really a veritable pocket tool kit. It possessed a standard blade, three saw blades, a screw driver, wire cutters and a can opener. It had steel handles and was blued throughout. There were no marks of any kind. Records relating to this type of equipment are still classified, and so identification is somewhat tenuous. The knife described and illustrated here, however, has been recognized by several veterans of the O.S.S., all of whom mentioned having seen it in kits during the war.

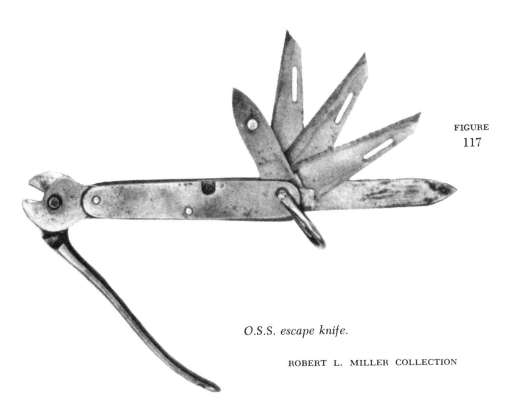

O.S.S. escape knife.

ROBERT L. MILLER COLLECTION

After the close of the war, the Office of the Chief of Ordnance made a study of the use of knives and bayonets by American troops. It has often been said, even by some veterans, that they never saw a knife used in action and that its only value was for opening C or K rations or other similar uses. The study found otherwise. It reported that the knife had been a definite morale factor and was apt to be retained when all other equipment was thrown away. And it stated further:

> Official records definitely establish that, in numerous instances, lives of servicemen were saved by reason of being armed with bayonets or trench knives, under circumstances where the use of any other type of weapon was precluded.
>
> In combat theaters where terrain, weather, or other conditions were favorable for enemy infiltration, it has been found that the bayonet and trench knife were the weapons most commonly used for disposing of enemy personnel who succeeded in penetrating outer defense lines. Those weapons had the great advantage of silence. Gunfire at night, the time when infiltration was most successful, betrayed position both by flashes and sound, besides disturbing the rest of nearly exhausted fighting men. Furthermore, it was frequently found the bayonet was the only weapon which could force enemy infantrymen to yield vital disputed positions.

The language is not dramatic, but it indicates that Ordnance understands the feeling of most combat soldiers that next to their rifle or carbine, their knife is their most valuable piece of equipment.

NAVAL DIRKS AND OTHER KNIVES

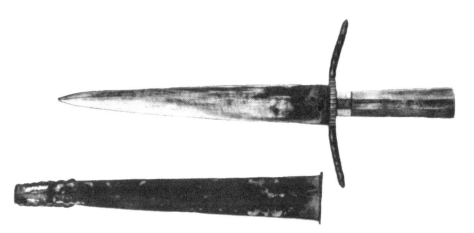

FIGURE
118

Dirk of Capt. Stephen Decatur.   U. S. NAVAL ACADEMY MUSEUM

Naval dirks and knives have always held a particular fascination for the student and collector of edged weapons. They bring with them the aura of romance that surrounds the sailing-ship era. They recall the heroics of the small American Navy during its formative years in wars with France, the Barbary pirates and England, in the trips of exploration and on through history to the present day. They are scarce enough to make collecting them a real challenge, but at the same time they afford a greater variety of types than any other single category.

The most colorful of all the naval knives is, of course, the dirk. As companion to and substitute for the sword, it combined the most fascinating characteristics of each. As part of an officer's uniform, it had all the decorative features of the sword. At the same time it was a short and sometimes efficiently designed weapon.

95

No one knows when dirks were first worn by American naval officers and midshipmen. They were first mentioned officially in the regulations of 1802 with the statement that they were not to be worn on shore. This seems to indicate that dirks were being worn at least at the time the regulations were written, and probably had been worn for some years previously, possibly since the Revolution.

The exact history of the dirk in the United States Navy after 1802 is also a bit vague. The regulations of November 23, 1813, required officers and midshipmen to wear cut and thrust swords with full dress but allowed them to wear dirks with their undress uniforms. Thereafter the regulations are silent on the subject of dirks for fifty-six years until 1869, when new regulations permitted midshipmen alone to wear them, and then only for boat duty. The regulations of 1869 are particularly important because the type of dirk is specified and illustrated. Prior to that time the choice of dirks had been left largely to the taste of the individual owner. Midshipmen retained the privilege of wearing dirks at least through 1876. The regulations of that year are the last to mention them, and presumably dirks were abandoned shortly thereafter.

Since the design of dirks prior to 1869 was left in the hands of the individual officers and midshipmen, a great variety of sizes and forms were used. Generally speaking, all were yellow-mounted. That is, the mounts of the hilt and scabbard were brass or gilt because yellow was the official color for Navy buttons and sword hilts. Some had straight blades, however, and some were sharply curved. Some were single-edged, some double-edged. And guards, grips and pommels came in infinite forms.

Despite this confusion, it is possible to date a given dirk with relative ease. This is done by reference to the few contemporary pictures which show dirks, by studying those dirks known to have been used by particular officers and most of all by comparing the workmanship and decoration with that found on contemporary swords. Frequently swords and dirks were made and sold as sets. In such cases at least one of them usually bears the maker's name, and that affords a further check on the date of the dirk's manufacture.

The earliest dirks seem to have been sturdy weapons with straight double-edged blades, resembling the early daggers. There is one of these in the museum of the United States Naval Academy at Annapolis which belonged to the renowned Captain Stephen Decatur. It has a wide blade, nine and three-eight inches long, ivory grips, large functional brass quillons and a brass scabbard. Decatur undoubtedly wore this dirk after 1800, but it is typical of those popular from the Revolution through the turn of the century.

Shortly after 1800 the curved blade began to appear, and it soon completely supplanted the straight double-edged blade. Most of these newer dirks were made in France or England. In contrast to the plain types that had preceded them, they were usually highly decorated. The pommel most often was cast in the form of an eagle's head, but some few had the bent French pistol-grip shape, and a few were simply covered with a convex cap decorated with leaves. The grips were bone or ivory or wood covered with plaques of mother-of-pearl. Usually they were fluted, ribbed or carved with spiral grooves. The guards bore dolphins, anchors or leaf decorations. The blades, which were sometimes as long as sixteen inches in a straight line from hilt to point, were normally blued for about two-thirds of their length and etched with American emblems, military trophies and floral sprays. A gold wash was then applied to the etching. The scabbards were sometimes made entirely of brass, but usually they were black leather with brass mounts. Normally dirks were worn suspended from the belt, and so there were two carrying rings on the scabbard as well as an occasional stud for a frog. All brass mounts on both scabbard and hilt were usually gilded.

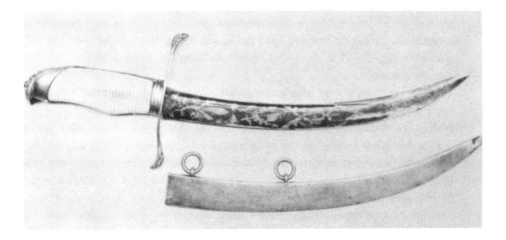

FIGURE
119

Dirk probably made by a Pennsylvania silversmith about 1800–05. Since this particular specimen is silver-mounted, it may have been carried by an Army officer, but the shape is typically naval. HERMANN W. WILLIAMS COLLECTION

FIGURE
120

Naval dirk made in France about 1800–05. Note the "pistol grip" pommel. The blade is 9¼ inches long.   U. S. NAVAL ACADEMY MUSEUM

As the years passed there were slight changes in the styles of decoration that help in determining when a specimen was made. The eagle head on the pommel became more sophisticated, and it developed a well-defined crest. The most noticeable change, however, took place in the blade decorations. A new style of etching became popular which left the subject area of bright steel with the surrounding background frosted. Shortly after 1820 panels with this new bright etching began to appear in the midst of the normal blued and gilded ornamentation. By 1830 most blades were decorated with the bright etching, and the blued and gilded blades were rapidly disappearing. By that time, however, the sharply curved blade had also largely vanished.

The supremacy of the curved-bladed dirk had been threatened as early as 1820 when the straight double-edged blade began to reappear. The blades on these new dirks differed from the straight blades of the earlier era in that they tended to be both longer and narrower. Occasionally they had a central fuller, and normally they were etched. Sometimes they were blued and gilded, but usually they had the latest bright etching. The eagle-head pommel disappeared. Most of these new dirks had bone or ivory grips and no real pommel at all. There were also some hilts made entirely of brass, and brass scabbards engraved with leaf and naval motifs became the rule. These straight-bladed dirks continued in use at least through the 1840's and apparently remained fashionable until the regulations of 1869 prescribed a standard model.

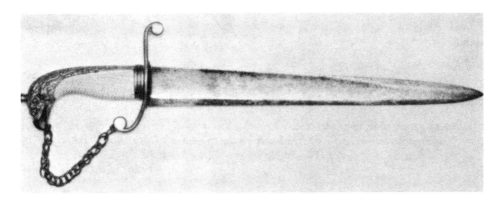

FIGURE
121

Naval dirk, 1808–16, with 13¾-inch blade. This dirk was probably made in England, but its matching sword bears the name of the dealer: Richard, Upson & Co. of New York.

HERMANN W. WILLIAMS COLLECTION

FIGURE
122

Naval dirk with 16-inch blade made in France, 1812–20. U. S. NATIONAL MUSEUM

FIGURE
123

Naval dirk, 1812–20, with 14¼-inch blade. HERMANN W. WILLIAMS COLLECTION

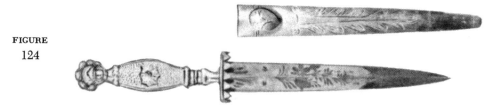

FIGURE
124

Small naval dirk of about 1820–24, which is said to have belonged to Edward Thayer, who served as a midshipman under the famed Capt. James Lawrence in the ill-fated Chesapeake. *The blade is only 5¾ inches long.*

U. S. NAVAL ACADEMY MUSEUM

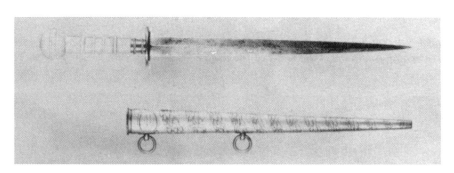

FIGURE
125

Naval dirk which belonged to Edward Trenchard, about 1822–24. The blade is 8⅝ inches long. U. S. NATIONAL MUSEUM

FIGURE
126

Naval dirk with 12-inch blade, 1825–35. Note the New York State crest engraved on the scabbard. LEONARD D. PELTON COLLECTION

FIGURE
127

Simple naval dirk, about 1830, which belonged to Capt. John Downes.

U. S. NAVAL ACADEMY MUSEUM

This so-called model of 1869 retained the straight double-edged blade. The main changes appeared in the hilt, which reflected contemporary taste. The eagle head returned to the pommel, but it was a crude and ugly casting. The guard was larger and more functional, decorated with engraving only. The grips were covered with sharkskin and bound with brass wire in the manner of the naval officers' sword. The scabbard was black leather with plain undecorated brass mounts. All in all, it was a simple weapon entirely suitable for the midshipman who now had the sole right to wear it and whose position in life did not yet require him to display a handsomer arm.

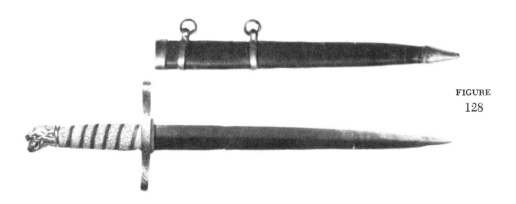

FIGURE
128

Naval dirk of the pattern of 1869.   U. S. NAVAL ACADEMY MUSEUM

So much for the dirk. Despite the fact that some were efficient weapons, it was primarily an ornament. Dirks may occasionally have been drawn in anger, but such occurrences must have been extremely rare. No record of the use of a dirk in combat seems to have survived.

There were other naval knives, however, which were strictly functional. In the days of sailing ships, every sailor needed a good knife. Ropes had to be cut and spliced, and various other odd jobs requiring a cutting blade were always waiting to be done. Whittling or carving was one of the sailor's principal amusements during long months at sea. And if a man became tangled in a running line, a good knife with which to cut himself free often meant the difference between life and death.

Most sailors carried clasp knives for these purposes. Merchant seamen and the crews of whalers usually bought their own. In the Navy these essential knives were issued to seamen at least as early as the Civil War. The first identifiable clasp knife issued by the Navy about the time of the Civil War was a jackknife in the classic sense. It had a single blade three and three-quarter inches long with a rounded almost beak point and was stamped "U.S. NAVY" on the reverse side. The handle was antler, and the bolster was forged iron. At the far end of the handle was a brass staple so that the knife could be carried on a lanyard. Apparently all of these knives were made in Sheffield and supplied to the Navy through an American jobber.

FIGURE
129

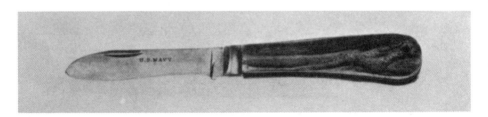

Navy jackknife of the Civil War period.   WILLIAM SHEMERLUK COLLECTION

During the 1870's or early 1880's the Navy began purchasing a clasp knife of a slightly different pattern. The size remained the same; the handle was still antler, the linings and bolster iron and the staple brass. But the blade swelled toward the end and terminated in a square "point." The "U.S. NAVY" stamp also was larger. All specimens of this knife available for examination were made by Cambridge & Co., England.

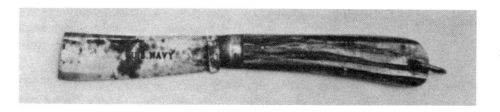

FIGURE
130

Navy jackknife of about 1870–90.   D. J. HARRILL COLLECTION

With the coming of the 1890's a third and last official clasp knife for sailing-ship duty made its appearance. It was strikingly different from its predecessors, with an absolutely rectangular blade that retracted into the handle and locked in position with a thumb catch on top. The blade was still marked "U.S. NAVY" on the reverse side, but it was an etched mark instead of a stamp. The grips were rectangular and made of bone gouged to resemble antler. The holster was iron, the linings brass and the staple was replaced by a screw eye.

The dating of these three knives is of necessity only approximate because the surviving records that relate to them are never specific and contain no descriptions.

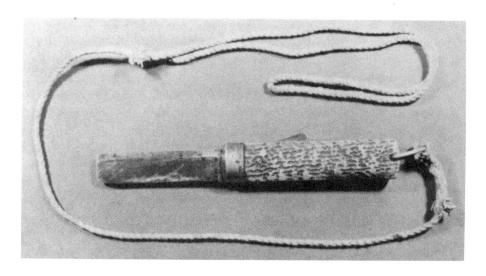

FIGURE
131

Navy pocketknife of the Spanish-American War era.

U. S. NAVAL ACADEMY MUSEUM

Even after the sailing-ship era, the Navy continued to issue pocket-knives to its seamen. These late knives, however, were of the type usually associated by most people with the Boy Scouts, technically known as utility knives, with master blade, can opener, screw driver and awl. They were still marked "U.S. NAVY" on the master blade, and the handles were still bone, sometimes carved to resemble antler, sometimes smooth. There were no longer specific tasks ·aboard ship requiring such knives, and they were provided primarily as a convenience for the personal use of the men.

Practice differed throughout the Navy. These pocketknives were theoretically issued to each man until 1949, but in many instances seamen were forced to purchase their own knives from Sea Stores or Ships' Service. In such instances, the knives available for sale varied all the way from the utility model described to a simple two-bladed jackknife. In Navy parlance, however, all were officially called "jackknives."

The last pocketknife officially issued by the Navy was adopted during World War II. It was entirely different from its predecessors both in purpose and design. Instead of being a tool for the repair of ropes and rigging or for personal convenience, this was an instrument for survival, and as such it was issued primarily to aviators as part of their survival kits. It was a large knife, six inches long when closed, and it had two blades, a standard knife blade four and three-quarter inches long pivoted at one end and a 5-inch saw blade at the other. There was a special lock for the knife blade to hold it rigid when fully open. The grips were black plastic, and all metal parts were blued. A small whetstone was also normally included in the kit with the knife.

The pocketknives carried by merchant seamen in the last century were normally single-bladed jackknives. The handles were sometimes wood, sometimes antler, bone or horn. As a rule they were simple and sturdy, and surviving specimens indicate that they were used long and hard. It is not unusual to find blades sharpened down to half their original thickness. Many ships' officers also carried pocketknives, and these were often of high quality. Among them, penknives and double-bladed jackknives were popular as well as the single-bladed jackknives favored by the crews.

There is one very interesting bit of folklore about seamen's clasp knives, and it may well be true. According to this tradition, men long at sea in confined quarters became quarrelsome and were apt to use their clasp knives to settle their disputes. In order to reduce the danger of may-

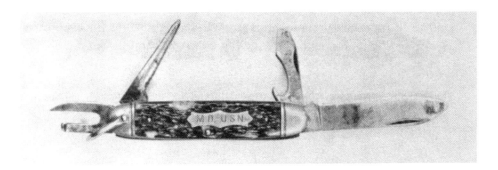

FIGURE
132

Modern Navy pocketknife. This particular specimen was issued to a medical corpsman and so has the letters "M.D.-U.S.N." on the escutcheon plate.
HAROLD FARNHAM COLLECTION

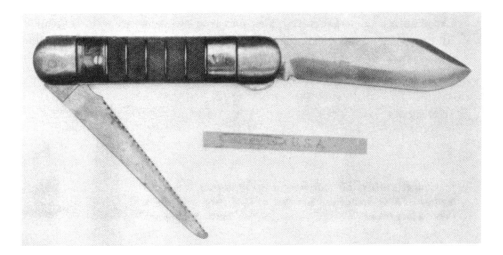

FIGURE
133

Survival-kit knife and whetstone for Navy pilots, World War II. AUTHOR'S COLLECTION

hem in such situations, the officers are supposed to have made a practice of breaking off the points of the men's knives to reduce their effectiveness as weapons.

Like most good folklore, this tale probably has a basis of fact. Certainly there is at least circumstantial evidence to support it. The great bulk of surviving seamen's knives from the last century are found with broken

FIGURE
134

Pocketknife carried by a Naval surgeon during the Civil War.

U. S. NAVAL ACADEMY MUSEUM

points. It is a rare one that retains its blade intact. The United States Navy also preferred a blade with a square "point" for some reason when a normal point would have made a number of tasks easier. True or not, it is at least plausible and an interesting topic for speculation.

Some men, both in the Regular Navy and the merchant marine, preferred sheath to pocketknives. This was true of officers as well as seamen. In these instances any contemporary knife was apt to be chosen. The smaller bowie types were probably the most popular, but some daggers and even butcher knives with homemade sheaths were also used.

Jackknives carried by merchant seamen during the 19th century. These knives are unusual in that they still retain their points intact. MYSTIC SEAPORT

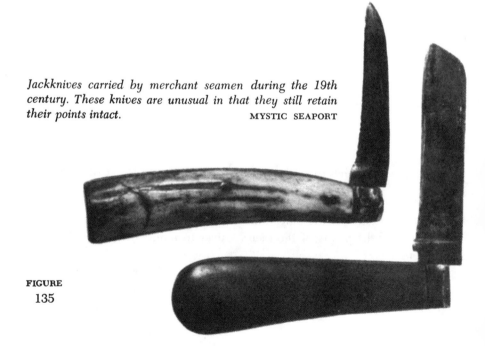

FIGURE
135

In addition to the utilitarian pocketknives, the Navy has also issued a few fighting knives to its enlisted men. The first known mention of such a knife occurs in the inventory of the Pensacola Navy Yard in 1829, which lists three "Boarding Knives." Just what these boarding knives looked like remains a mystery. No other documentary reference has been found, and no surviving specimen has been identified. Their purpose, however, is crystal clear. Seamen at that time were normally issued axes, pikes and cutlasses when they set out to board and capture an enemy ship. In such hand-to-hand actions, where struggling men were crammed into the narrow confines of a ship's deck, a large knife would have been an eminently useful weapon.

It was probably such a purpose that Admiral John A. Dahlgren had in mind in 1856 when he presented his views on the ideal bayonet for naval use:

> The present bayonet, which is the most useless thing in the world except at the end of a musket, may be replaced by another, fashioned like a stout sword or bowie knife, which will be quite as serviceable for its particular purpose and useful in many others besides.

To illustrate his theory, Dahlgren devised a heavy bayonet which was later adopted as official and used with the so-called Plymouth rifle, another weapon also manufactured according to Dahlgren's specifications. These new bowie bayonets were made under contract by the Ames Manufacturing Company at Chicopee Falls, Massachusetts, and were unique in the history of American naval small arms. The heavy blade was eleven and seven-

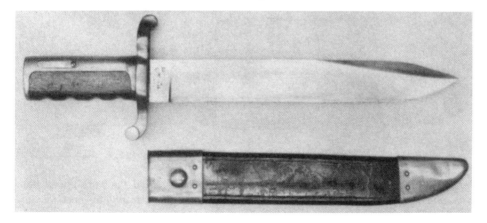

FIGURE
136

Dahlgren bowie bayonet.   AUTHOR'S COLLECTION

eighths inches long and one and five-eighths inches wide, with a semispear point. It was stamped on the obverse side with the date of manufacture and on the reverse with the Ames mark. The guard was brass, and there was a heavy brass strip along the back of the walnut grips and over the pommel. The scabbard was black leather with brass throat and tip. All in all it was a massive weapon that felt well in the hand but made a rifle terribly muzzle-heavy when used as a bayonet.

After the Dahlgren, the Navy issued no more fighting knives until World War II. The various Army bolos were frequently carried among landing stores after their adoption but were not normally issued on a regular basis. During the war, however, the Navy adopted two models and designated them the Mark 1 and Mark 2. The M 1 was a short knife similar to the standard commercial hunting knife. It was not big enough for fighting and not stout enough for heavy duty. The men to whom it was issued in the Pacific theater usually traded it off to the native islanders. The M 2 was a good knife. It had a six-and-seven-eighths-inch blade with a clipped point and a short but wide central fuller. The cross guard and pommel were iron, and the grips were built up of leather washers. The obverse side of the blade bore the stamp of the Camillus Cutlery Company of New York, and the reverse was marked "U.S.N./MARK 2." The scabbard was gray plastic

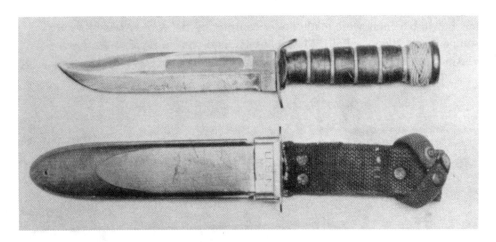

FIGURE
137

Navy Mark 2 knife. The frogman who used this specimen added the Turk's-head braid so he could recognize his own knife and bent the cross guard to obtain more leverage with his thumb. TOM DOYLE COLLECTION

with an iron throat and a web belt loop. The outside of the throat was stamped "USN/MK2."

The Mark 2 was issued primarily to two groups of seamen: shore personnel at advanced bases and frogmen. It was particularly important to the frogmen. In their underwater demolition work they frequently needed a knife to cut fuses, ropes and the like. Also they often encountered enemy frogmen who had been sent down to intercept them. When that happened, a weird noiseless battle would take place in the half-light of the depths or sometimes in almost complete darkness. In these grim struggles a knife was the only possible weapon, and a good one often meant victory and survival. Men detailed for boat duty also usually carried the M 2, and in some instances, at the whim of the commanding officer, everyone on board his ship might be required to wear it.

In addition to the frogmen for shallow underwater work, the Navy also had and still maintains a staff of deep-sea divers. These men, wearing diving suits and helmets, work at greater depths and in colder water than the lightly equipped frogmen. They also use a highly specialized knife. The Navy has no special deep-sea diver's knife of its own. It merely purchases those that it needs from regular commercial outlets. These knives possess exceptionally sturdy blades, usually six and one-half inches long. One side has a normal edge; the other has saw teeth. The grips are turned

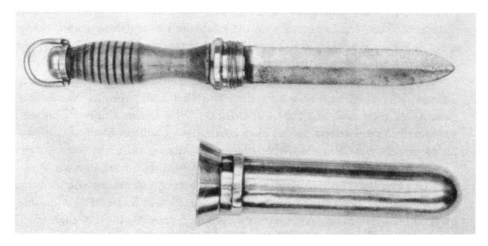

FIGURE
138

Deep-sea diver's knife.   WILLIAM SHEMERLUK COLLECTION wood, and there is a brass pommel with a staple for a lanyard. Between the grips and the blade there is a brass shoulder with threads so that the knife may be screwed into its heavy cylindrical brass scabbard. The scabbard is attached to the diving suit by passing a strap through a fixed staple on one side of the throat.

These were the principal knives used by the Navy and by merchant seamen. There is also one separate and most interesting category which must be considered within this general grouping: the knives of the Marine Corps. The Marines obtain some of their arms from the Navy, some from the Army, and some they purchase themselves. Always a relatively small organization, their distinctive arms are correspondingly few in number, and consequently more difficult for the collector to obtain.

Because of their very special duties, the Marines have been among the last of the original branches of the service to carry knives officially. Their duties aboard ship and at various bases did not require them, and thus the choice of carrying a personally purchased knife was left to the individual. The twentieth century, however, brought extensive duty in the Pacific, Central America and the Caribbean under conditions that made a knife a necessity. At first, Army knives, especially the bolos, were used, but with the advent of World War II, the Marines adopted some models of their own.

The first specifically Marine Corps fighting knife was identical with the Navy Mark 2 except for the marks on the blade. Marine Corps knives were stamped "U.S.M.C.," originally on the blade, and later, because such stamping tended to weaken the blade, on the cross guard. The Marines also preferred a leather scabbard to the Navy's gray plastic.

This weapon was officially called the "fighting-utility knife," but to almost all veterans it was known as the "KA-BAR" because the earliest examples they saw had that trade-mark of the Union Cutlery Company stamped in large letters on the blade. Later, the Camillus Cutlery Company also made some. The date when these new knives were first issued is not known, but it was probably late in 1942. By 1943 they were in general use.

Also in 1943, Marine Raider units were issued a stiletto copied after the Sykes-Fairbirn design used by British Commandos. It had a straight double-edged blade seven and one-quarter inches long etched with the name of the manufacturer and had the letters "U.S.M.C." in a scroll. All specimens examined were made by the Camillus Cutlery Company of New York. Unlike its British prototype, the Marine Corps stiletto had a cast-aluminum

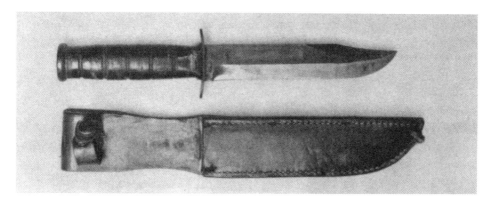

FIGURE
139

Marine Corps fighting-utility "Ka-Bar" knife.   JAMES ROBINSON COLLECTION

hilt to avoid the use of brass, which was a strategic material. The scabbard was leather with an iron plate at the tip to prevent injury in case of a fall or other accident.

In addition to the Raiders, other officers and some enlisted men were offered the stiletto. None of the Marines liked them, however, because their blades were too light and brittle for all-purpose work and because they were designed so specifically for stabbing that they restricted the number of possible attacks and parries. As a result, most Marines who got them either turned them back or stowed them away in their sea bags while they used the KA-BAR or one of the many privately purchased or personally manufactured knives for which the Marines were famous.

Most of the privately purchased or specially made knives that the Marines used were similar to those carried by soldiers and described in the previous chapter. In at least one instance, however, a whole Raider battalion arranged for special knives of an irregular pattern. The famous 2nd or Carlson's Raiders procured a knife with a heavy blade and clipped point. Its grips were wood, and the guard was brass despite the scarcity of that metal. It was a good knife, and the 2nd Raiders were particularly proud of it because it was different and distinctive.

With the Marines as with the Army, the development of the M 4 bayonet-knife brought an end to all other official fighting knives for troops armed with the carbine. As already mentioned, this new model was adopted in July, 1944, and supplies began to reach the Marine Corps by the end of that year.

Marine Corps stiletto.   COL. DONALD L. DICKSON COLLECTION

During World War II, Navy Medical Corpsmen serving with the Marines also carried a special knife. These corpsmen's knives were purchased by the Marine Corps rather than by the Navy, and they were listed on the company inventories instead of being issued to the individual corpsmen who carried them in scabbards on their packs. At first, standard Army bolos of the models 1917 and 1917CT seem to have been used, but later new patterns with round, clipped or squared points and heavy blades twelve and three-eighths inches long were developed. Some had guards. Some did not, but the grips were always roughly cut wooden scales. These corpsmen's knives were marked on the blade with the initials "U.S.M.C." and the name or trade-mark of the maker, usually "CHATILLON" or "VILLAGE BLACKSMITH." The Marines always accused the corpsmen of using these cleaverlike knives to amputate limbs or for other macabre purposes. Actually they were intended for clearing brush, erecting shelters, fashioning makeshift litters, splints and other such uses. As such, they were the lineal descendants of the Army Hospital Corps knives but sturdier and much more useful.

The final Marine Corps knife to be issued was a pocket knife. It apparently first reached troops in the field late in 1945. Any man in the Corps

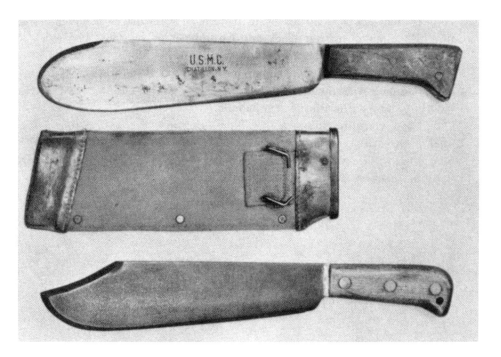

FIGURE
141

Marine Corps medical corpsmen's knives. The lower specimen has lost its guard; the upper one never had any. NORM FLAYDERMAN AND AUTHOR'S COLLECTIONS

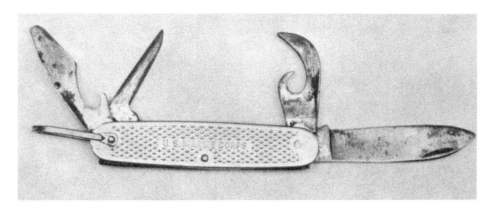

FIGURE
142

Modern Marine Corps pocketknife. AUTHOR'S COLLECTION

who wanted one was entitled to it. In form, it was what cutlers would call the utility model—master blade and can opener on one end, and awl and combination screw driver and bottle opener on the other. The linings were brass, and the handles were aluminum. There were no bolsters, but there was a staple for a lanyard. The only mark was the legend "U. S. MARINE CORPS" stamped on the reverse handle.

These were the knives of the Navy, Marine Corps and merchant seamen. From dirk to pocketknife, from stiletto to bolo, they represented within one framework a wide variety of tools and weapons. No other single category in American knife collecting offers so much diversity.

THE INDIAN AND HIS KNIFE

FIGURE
143

Pre-Columbian stone knife found in a cave in Dinosaur National Monument. The original haft is lashed to the blade. UNIVERSITY OF COLORADO MUSEUM

T HE first people to use knives on the North American Continent were, of course, the Indians; and they were using them centuries before the first Europeans set foot on these shores. They were crude and ineffective knives, it is true, made of stone, hard wood, animal teeth or bones, or, in some cases, copper. But they were the first knives used in what is now the United States.

Before the coming of the white man, the Indian used his knife primarily as a tool, not as a weapon. The early explorers and colonists who found the Indians in their primitive state were much interested in their weapons. Their journals, letters and accounts described them in detail, but none of them mention knives as weapons. Instead they list only the bow and arrow, the dart or spear and the club or "sword." When knives are mentioned it is strictly as utensils, and specialized knives are listed for different kinds of work.

One of the best descriptions of these early knives is given by Captain John Smith, who was a careful observer as well as a resourceful soldier. **115**

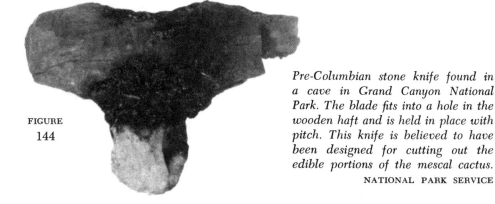

FIGURE
144

Pre-Columbian stone knife found in a cave in Grand Canyon National Park. The blade fits into a hole in the wooden haft and is held in place with pitch. This knife is believed to have been designed for cutting out the edible portions of the mescal cactus.

NATIONAL PARK SERVICE

FIGURE
145

Copper knife blade from Wisconsin.   WEST POINT MUSEUM

In writing about the Virginia Indians of 1612, he not only indicates two of the kinds of knife in use but also how important they were in the Indian's life:

> For his knife he hath the splinter of a reed to cut his feathers in forme. With this knife also, he will joint a Deare or any beast, shape his shooes, buskins, mantels, &c. To make the nock of his arrow hee hath the tooth of a Bever set in a sticke, wherewith he grateth it by degrees.

Shortly after the European colonists arrived they began to trade with the Indians. They needed the red man's corn to supplement their own meager food supplies in the early years, and they wanted his furs because of the price they brought back home. Being sharp businessmen, they soon noticed that one of the things the Indians wanted most was a European steel knife. This was easily supplied, and the new knives quickly spread across the country as the colonists traded them to the Indians and these in turn traded them to other Indians.

These new steel knives had a profound effect on the Indian's way of life. With a good sharp knife he could make things that were impossible or too laborious with stone knives. The knife had been an indispensable tool before. It became more so now. And it became a favorite weapon.

The rapidity of this change is illustrated by an incident in Massachusetts in 1623. Miles Standish, the doughty little warrior of Plymouth, had been sent to Wessagusset by the Pilgrim Fathers to quell some reported Indian disturbances. The Indians knew why he had come, and they sharpened their knives in front of him and made insulting speeches and gestures. Two of them, Pecksuot and Wituwamat, especially taunted him about it. Wituwamat bragged about his knife, which had a woman's head on the pommel, adding, "But I have another at home wherewith I have killed both French and English. And that hath a man's face on it and, by and by these two must marry. . . ." Pecksuot, who was a huge man compared to the diminutive Standish, twitted the sensitive captain about his size and fingered a knife which hung on a cord about his neck, "the point whereof he had made as sharp as a needle and ground the back also to an edge."

Standish bore the insults as long as he could. Finally he lured these two braves along with two of their companions into a room with himself and three of his soldiers. At Standish's signal the door was locked, and the little captain sprang at the huge Pecksuot, seized his carefully honed knife and, after a violent struggle, killed him with it. Standish's three followers took care of Wituwamat and the other two Indians. This was only three years after the landing of the Pilgrims, but already the Indians were relying on the knife as a weapon.

It is impossible to be sure from these descriptions exactly what kind of knives the Indians had. Obviously one had originally been single-edged before it had been sharpened by Pecksuot. The other had a sculptured pommel and was quite probably a French quillon dagger of the type which immediately preceded the plug bayonet. Early French plug bayonets often had heads sculptured on the pommel and the ends of the quillons. Indeed, the earliest known European knife definitely used by an Indian was just this type of plug bayonet with helmeted male heads on the pommel and quillon terminals. This knife was taken from an Indian killed during a raid on Deerfield, Massachusetts, in 1675, and it is now on display there.

Almost all types of knives were traded to the Indians at one time or another. Archaeologists digging in graves have recovered a great variety of

FIGURE
146

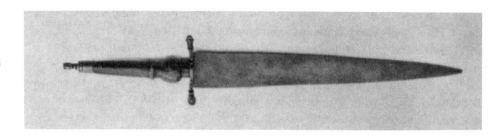

Plug bayonet taken from an Indian who was using it as a knife in 1675.

MEMORIAL HALL, DEERFIELD

FIGURE
147

Bone-handled knives excavated from Indian village sites of the late 17th and early 18th centuries.   ROCHESTER MUSEUM OF ARTS AND SCIENCES

pocket- and sheath knives. Where they exist, the records of trading companies also bear out the diversity of types kept in stock. The accounts of John Johnston, for instance, include the following entries during the years 1802–1811:

5 doz. Scalping knives—4 sizes	£ 8/13/9
1 doz. pen knives	3/9/6
1 doz. Barlow knives	10/2
2 9/12 doz. Jack knives @ 15/	2/1/3
6 doz. butcher knives @ 8/6	2/11
2 doz. 4-bladed pen knives	$9.33

The pen, Barlow and jackknives were, of course, the standard pocket-knives of the period. Perhaps because he had no pockets, the Indian was never as fond of these as he was of the fixed-bladed knives. Also, the other knives were bigger and more useful for a greater variety of jobs, especially for heavy-duty cutting and for fighting.

The term "scalping knife" has always appealed to the popular imagination. It calls forth pictures of a savage and grisly practice just far enough removed from everyday experience to acquire an aura of romance and color. Actually there was no special type of knife used primarily for scalping. Almost any kind of knife could be used, although a narrow blade was preferable to a wide one.

Briefly, the technique of scalping was this. The Indian seized his fallen opponent's hair. Lifting it up, he made an incision across the forehead below the hair line. As he lengthened this cut, he continued to pull on the hair and work his blade up under the scalp, easing its separation from the skull. When the trophy was completely freed he would shake it a few times and perhaps wipe it on the grass. Then he would slip it under his belt or into his pouch and take it home for curing.

No one knows how or when the practice of scalping began. De Soto's men observed it among the Southern Indians in 1539, and other early explorers reported it elsewhere. At that time it must have been done with stone or wooden knives. Steel knives made the job easier and were universally used for it when they were available. Because the blades of butcher and carving knives were best suited for the purpose—just as they were for any other form of skinning—they were the preferred type. But any good knife would do, and soon all Indian sheath knives became known as scalping knives.

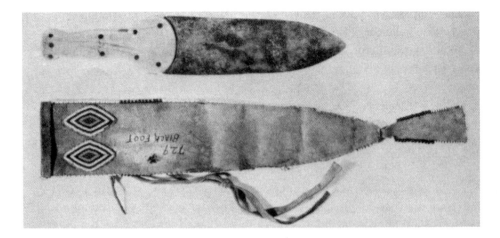

FIGURE
148

Indian knife of the type known as the beaver tail or stabber collected among the Black-feet in the 1840's. The handle is made of two pieces of bone held together with copper rivets. SMITHSONIAN INSTITUTION

The seventeenth and early eighteenth centuries saw metal knives spread rapidly among the Indians of the East, South and Southwest. The tribes of the Great Plains, the Rocky Mountains and the Pacific Northwest were among the last to obtain them, but before 1800 even these remote Indians began to acquire the white man's keen knife in quantity. At first these were obtained by trading with tribes farther east or south. Then direct contact was made with traders from Canada representing British fur companies and finally, with agents of American firms.

The early knives in the Northwest were thus predominantly English. Many kinds were introduced, but only two became really popular. These were the single-edged butcher or carving knife and the dagger. The butcher knives were generally similar to the later varieties made by the John Russell Company and described elsewhere, but some of them had considerably broader blades than the later American knives. The daggers were a distinct form. Known various as the "Hudson's Bay dag," the "beaver-tail knife" or the "stabber," they were a favorite weapon for hand-to-hand combat, particularly among the Blackfoot and related groups. The blades of these heavy knives were double-edged and very broad. Apparently they were traded to the Indians without handles, for all known specimens show Indian hilts.

The modern student of knife-fighting would reject these daggers as clumsy and inefficient. They would be for scientific fighting. But the Indian had his own techniques. He held his knife with the blade below the hand, much like the European three centuries before, and he concentrated on two principal blows—a powerful downward chopping motion aimed behind his opponent's collarbone or a sidewise stroke aimed at the ribs or stomach. With only these two attacks the Indian was an easy prey to a skilled knife-handler. But mostly he used his knife against other Indians, and they fought in the same manner as he.

Knife collected from unspecified Indians near the Missouri River before 1850. The spiral grooves of the wooden handle were originally wrapped with copper wire. The sheath is decorated with both glass and shell beads. SMITHSONIAN INSTITUTION   FIGURE 149

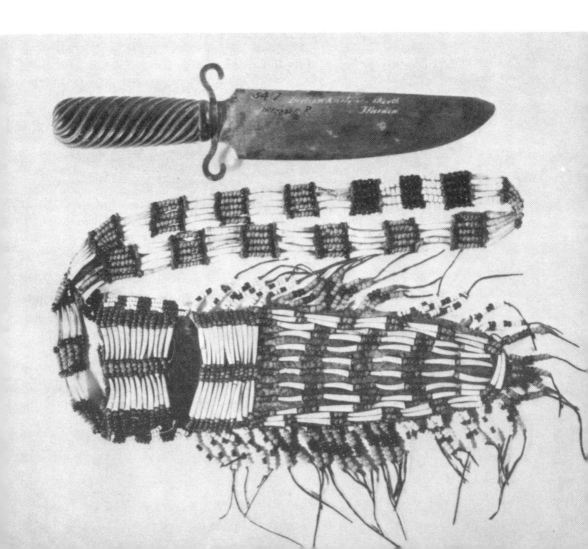

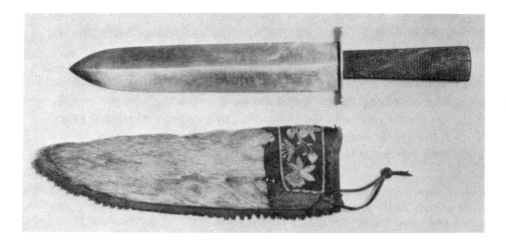

FIGURE
150

Knife made by Lowcock of 38 Cornhill (London?), about 1840, with 8½-inch double-edged blade. The sheath was made about the same time by an eastern Indian, judging by the decoration. It is made of deer hide, ornamented with red woolen cloth, porcupine quill work on a strip of leather at the throat and glass beads.

WILLIAM SHEMERLUK COLLECTION

FIGURE
151

Sioux knife with 10¼-inch blade, brass guard and antler handle wrapped with deer hide.

SMITHSONIAN INSTITUTION

By the 1840's American knives began to displace the English blades. The John Russell Company's "Green River" knives and similar types produced by such firms as Lamson & Goodnow soon dominated the field and held first place until the fur trade ceased shortly after the Civil War. Some of them even found their way up into Canada and Alaska.

In addition to these ready-made knives obtained from traders, the Indians also had some steel knives which they made themselves. Most of these seem to date after 1850, but some could well have been made earlier. Usually the blades were fashioned from files or saws, and the handles made

Roman Nose, a noted warrior of the Southern Cheyenne, painted from life by H. H. Cross. Here he holds his knife in the typical Indian fighting grip. Roman Nose was active in the Indian wars of 1864–68 and was killed in the Beecher's Island fight, 1868.

FIGURE 153

Conquering Bear of the Brulé Sioux painted from life by H. H. Cross. Note the broad-bladed knife. Legend has it that Conquering Bear lured Wild Bill Hickok into a Choctaw ambush from which Hickok miraculously escaped to track down his betrayer and kill him in a knife duel.

FIGURE 152

FIGURE
154

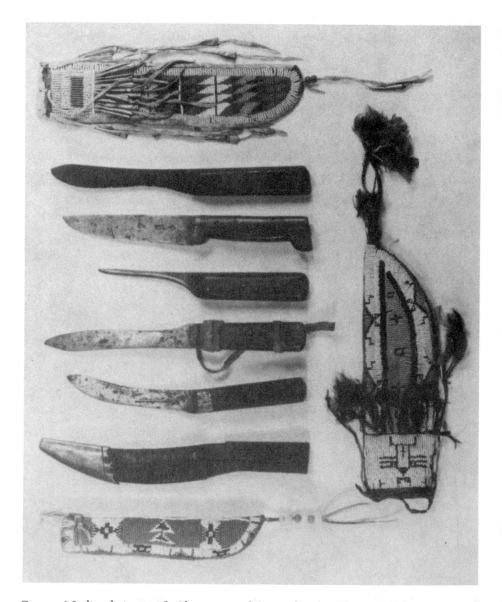

Group of Indian knives with Cheyenne and Sioux sheaths. The second knife is French and evidently came down from Canada. The bottom knife is a typical John Russell "Green River" skinning knife of about 1850. MARY R. DU MONT COLLECTION

of antler or bone. Often the grips were wrapped with deerskin, and usually there was no guard or other metal mounting on the hilt.

Like the mountain men, the Indians also made one universal alteration to the knives they planned to use for skinning. They ground off the original edge and made a new one with the bevel all on one side. They too found that this made skinning easier.

The Indian usually carried his knife in a sheath, either on his waist belt or suspended around his neck. The usual everyday sheath of the Plains Indians was made of leather with a wide flap studded with brass or copper rivets. At the top of this flap was a slot through which the belt was threaded before it passed over the main body of the scabbard. For ceremonial occasions there were handsomely beaded sheaths. Interestingly, almost all Indian scabbards were made deep enough to enclose the whole knife, handle and all.

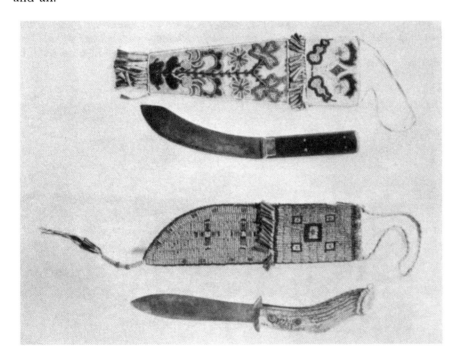

FIGURE
155

Two Plains Indian knives. The upper specimen is a skinning knife by Lamson & Goodnow, about 1860–70, with a 6-inch blade. The lower roughly-forged knife has a 6¼-inch blade including the guard which is fashioned from it.

SMITHSONIAN INSTITUTION

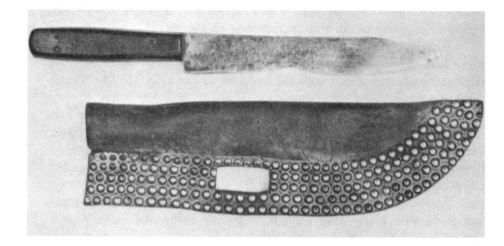

FIGURE
156

John Russell "Green River" butcher knife of about 1870–80 with typical everyday leather sheath studded with brass tacks popular among the Blackfoot and related tribes.

WILLIAM SHEMERLUK COLLECTION

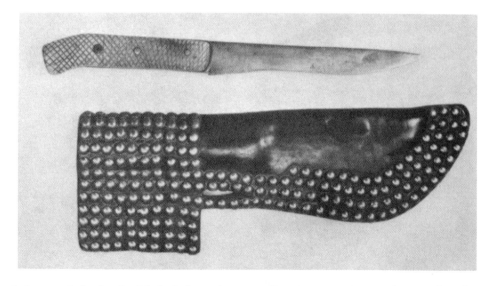

FIGURE
157

Indian-made knife, the blade fashioned from a file; the grips, bone. This also has the typical leather sheath studded with tacks.   GERALD FOX COLLECTION

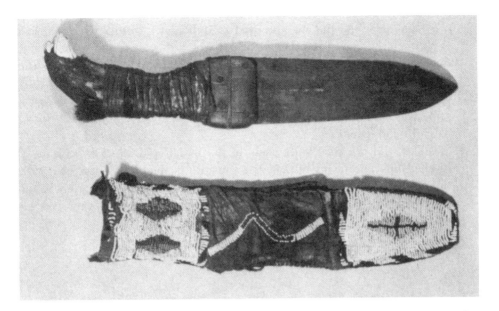

FIGURE
158

Bear-cult knife and sheath of the Blackfoot Indians. The blade is of the-beaver tail or stabber type. The grips are made from the jawbone of a bear.

MUSEUM OF THE AMERICAN INDIAN, HEYE FOUNDATION

In addition to their ordinary uses, some Indian knives were also connected with ceremonial and religious functions. Typical of these is the bear knife, used by members of the Bear Cult among the Assiniboin, Eastern Dakota, Blackfoot and Sarsi tribes. This knife usually possessed a trade steel blade, but it was hilted with the jawbones of a bear. It was a sacred object, used in ceremonials and carried into battle. Obtaining such a knife was difficult. When one was transferred to a new owner it involved a ritualistic ceremonial. Among the Blackfoot this provided a particularly severe test for the new candidate. As the ceremony drew to a close, the owner of the knife, after imitating the antics of a bear, would suddenly hurl the knife at the candidate. If he failed to catch it, he was not thought worthy of the sacred object. If he did catch it, he was thrown naked upon a bed of thorns and beaten thoroughly with the flat of the blade while the ceremonial paint was applied to his aching body.

Sometimes the Indians also used knife blades for other purposes. This is particularly true of the dagger blades which they acquired without handles. One frequently encounters them mounted in clubs or serving as spear points. Indeed their design rendered them even better suited for these purposes than for use as knives. The later knives were sometimes used the same way, too, and thus Green River knife blades are occasionally found on clubs and lances.

Thus did the steel knife come to the Indian and affect his culture. It reached him late in his history as a separate people, but it spread rapidly through all the tribes, easing and speeding almost all aspects of his handiwork. And it added a new weapon to his arsenal while it improved the efficiency of old ones.

POCKETKNIVES

FIGURE
159

Early 17th-century pocketknife found at Jamestown. It has one blade as well as a small cup for measuring powders and so may well have belonged to one of the first apothecaries in the colony. U. S. NATIONAL MUSEUM

Oﬀ ALL the forms of knives, the pocketknife has perhaps been man's most universal companion. Excavated specimens from Roman sites indicate that the folding pocketknife was popular at least as early as the first century A.D. In its infinite variations it is the possession of almost every man today. For centuries it has been both a household neighbor and the comrade of soldiers and sailors; the small boy's dream and the comfort of the aged whittler.

Throughout its history it has been known by a variety of names—clasp knife, pocketknife, jackknife, Barlow knife and penknife are a few of the commonest. Some of these are general terms. Some refer to specific designs.

One of the commonest of the specific names is "jackknife." It is also one of the oldest. European documents record the name as early as 1672, and it is probably much older. It occurs frequently in American colonial documents, and during the Revolution at least two states, New York and New Hampshire, required their militia to carry one. British and French soldiers also carried jackknives during that war, and many have been recovered from various forts and camp sites.

129

The exact origin and the original meaning of the name are unknown. Early versions and variants include Jockteleg knife, Jock the Leg Knife, Jactaleg knife, Jackleg knife, and dozens of others. As early as 1776 the famed etymologist Lord Haile was speculating about its derivation, and he thought he had solved the problem. He wrote ". . . the etymology of this word remained unknown till not many years ago an old knife was found having the inscription *Jacques de Liége*, the name of the cutler." From this beginning he reasoned that the name evolved to Jock de Leg, to Jackleg and was finally shortened to just plain jack. Other students of word origins followed Lord Haile's lead, and this story of its origin has been repeated ever since, though modern research has failed thus far to find evidence of any such cutler at Liége.

The early jackknives were apparently large knives with only one blade. Among the eighteenth-century specimens studied, the smallest was four inches long when closed, and most were five, six and one-half or seven inches. During the nineteenth century a smaller pen blade was often added, and today almost all jackknives have two blades. Both are on the same end of the knife, however, and this still remains the characteristic of the jack-knife: a large knife with not more than two blades, both pivoted at the same end.

Another pocketknife well known to history and legend is the Barlow. Actually the Barlow is a kind of jackknife. Supposedly a cutler named Barlow designed the knife in an attempt to produce a rugged knife at the cheapest possible price. To cut costs the blade was forged from high carbon steel, and the handle was usually made of bone with little effort spent in polishing or other finishing. To add strength, the bolster was increased in length and weight since that is the point of greatest strain on all folding knives. Generally speaking, the bolster of a Barlow should be about one-third of the length of the closed knife. Today Barlows have lost their original rough finish and their cheap price. Also there are often two blades, but the distinctive long bolster is still always present.

Whether a man named Barlow actually designed the knife is impossible to determine. But it has had a long and fascinating history. The name seems to have been adopted sometime in the seventeenth century. It is mentioned in American records at least as early as 1779 and seems to have been in general usage at that time. Because of its low price it was very popular among the working classes, and it was a great favorite with boys for many generations. John Russell is often credited with having been the first Amer-

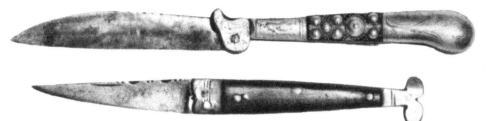

FIGURE
160

Two folding knives of the late 17th century. The upper specimen has a silver handle with a strip of black enamel in the center. The lower knife has a horn handle with brass mounts. GEORGE KERNODLE COLLECTION

FIGURE
161

Jackknives excavated from American Revolutionary camp sites near West Point. WEST POINT MUSEUM

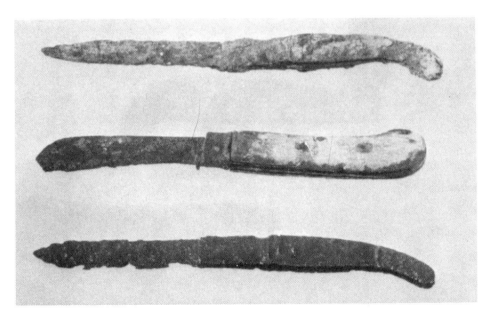

FIGURE
162

Jackknives excavated from the Revolutionary War camp sites of the British 17th Regiment at Inwood, N. Y. NEW-YORK HISTORICAL SOCIETY

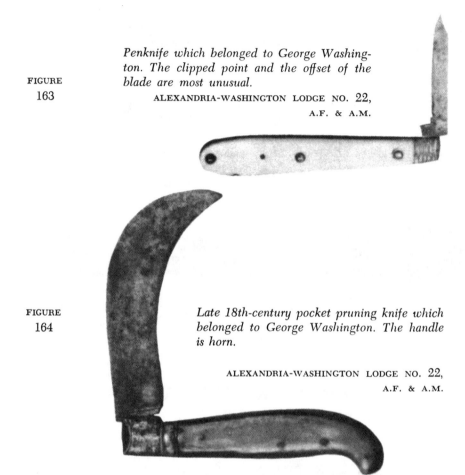

FIGURE
163

Penknife which belonged to George Washington. The clipped point and the offset of the blade are most unusual.

ALEXANDRIA-WASHINGTON LODGE NO. 22,
A.F. & A.M.

FIGURE
164

Late 18th-century pocket pruning knife which belonged to George Washington. The handle is horn.

ALEXANDRIA-WASHINGTON LODGE NO. 22,
A.F. & A.M.

FIGURE
165

Penknife which belonged to Thomas Jefferson. Family tradition states that he customarily used this knife to scrape the mud from his boots.

THOMAS JEFFERSON MEMORIAL FOUNDATION

ican cutler to manufacture Barlow knives, but that is by no means certain. Beyond doubt, however, is the fact that the Russell Barlow gained immortality through Mark Twain's Tom Sawyer and Huckleberry Finn, who treasured that knife as one of their most prized possessions. Many a man today who acquired his first knife before 1920 can well understand their enthusiasm for that sturdy blade.

The penknife derived from the need for a small, easily handled knife for trimming the goose or turkey quill pens which were universally used for writing before the invention of the steel pen a century ago. Usually these were lightly constructed and less than three inches long when folded. Interestingly, the penknife seems to have been the first to have been commonly produced with more than one blade. Two- and four-bladed models are mentioned as early as the eighteenth century.

About the middle of the last century an age of specialization in pocketknives set in, and the number of types began to multiply. There were farriers' knives which added stone hooks and sometimes hoof files to the standard blade; sailors' knives with marlin spikes; stock and cattle knives with blades at both ends; veterinarians' knives with fleams for bleeding and sometimes castrating blades; fish knives with scalers. The older pruning knives with their hooked blades were joined by budding and grafting knives. And more recently there have come plumbers' and electricians' knives as well as many others.

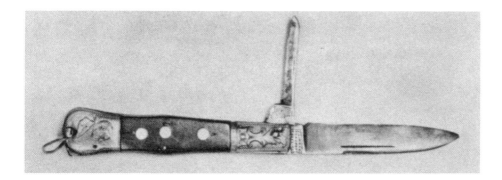

FIGURE
166

Two-bladed jackknife of about 1848–50, made by J. Lingard, Sheffield. The handles are wood, and the German silver mount opposite the bolster bears a picture, presumably of Zachary Taylor, with the words "OLD Z(?)ACK/I ASK NO FAVORS & OWN NO RESPONSIBILITIES." *The staple added by one of the knife's owners has obscured several of the letters.* WILLIAM SHEMERLUK COLLECTION

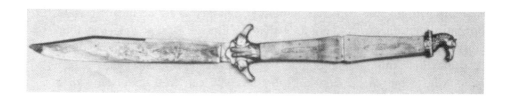

FIGURE
167

Huge folding knife with an 11-inch blade made by Unwin & Rodgers, Sheffield, 1850–60. The grips are horn; the mountings, German silver. The blade is etched with an eagle and the usual patriotic mottoes; also the words "California Knife" and "The Patriot's Self Defender."   WILLIAM SHEMERLUK COLLECTION

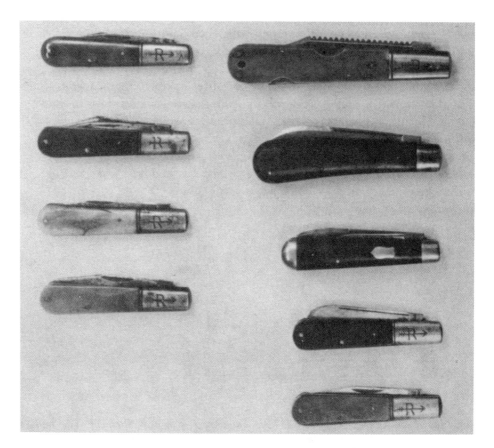

FIGURE
168

Pocketknives made by the John Russell Company during the 1860's. Those with the long bolsters are the famous Russell Barlows. All have wood, horn or bone handles.
JOHN S. DU MONT COLLECTION

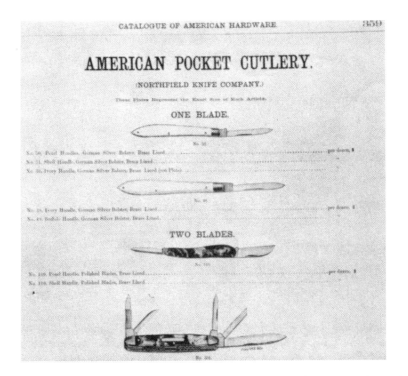

A group of American-made knives offered for sale in Russell and Irwin's catalog of 1865. Within a few years many other catalogs appeared with long pages of American pocketknives.

BELLA C. LANDAUER COLLECTION, NEW-YORK HISTORICAL SOCIETY

FIGURE
169

Actually there has been relatively little evolution in the design of the pocketknife since the seventeenth century. The major changes have come in the number and diversity of blades and in the use of different materials. As early as the Roman era bone and ivory, sometimes dyed green, were popular materials for handles. As late as 1800 they were still the most widely used, but they had been joined by metal (usually iron, brass, gold or silver), horn, wood and, on rare occasions, pearl and tortoise shell. Sometimes antler is also encountered, but it is usually associated with nineteenth-century knives. After 1870 the synthetics and plastics begin to appear, eventually supplanting the natural materials. Aluminum also joins the metals, first as an expensive novelty and then in the present century as a commoner material. For a short period about the turn of the century cheap metal castings often with commemorative or souvenir decorations finished

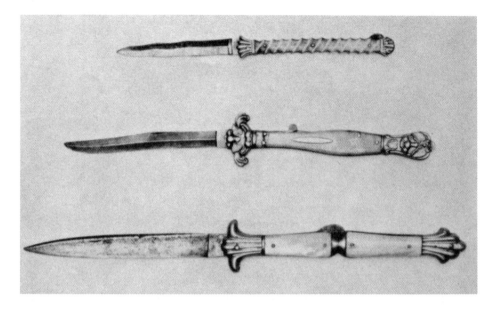

FIGURE
170

Group of folding dirk knives, made about 1850–60 for both general utility and self-defense. The blades range in length from 3½ to 6 inches. The handles are pearl, bone and ivory, and the mountings are German silver.   WILLIAM SHEMERLUK COLLECTION

usually in bronze or silver were popular for handles. Less noticeable among the material changes are the use of die-stamped brass for linings; the plating of the iron bolsters first with nickel in the middle 1800's and then with chrome or even the substitution of aluminum after 1900; and finally a shift from carbon steel to chrome steel for blades, which took place generally in America following the close of the first World War.

The metamorphosis of the pocketknife from a simple cutting instrument to an all-purpose pocket tool kit began shortly before 1850. Prior to that time a knife might have up to four different blades, but they were simple blades—possibly a general-purpose blade, a pen blade, or maybe even a pruning blade or a fleam. Eighteenth- and even seventeenth-century knives which could be converted to forks or spoons are also known, but that is about the extent of the variations. After 1825, however, the gadgeteer's ingenuity triumphed. There appeared stone hooks, buttonhooks, leather punches and awls, corkscrews, saws, screw drivers, scissors, files, can openers, bottle openers and others in infinite variety.

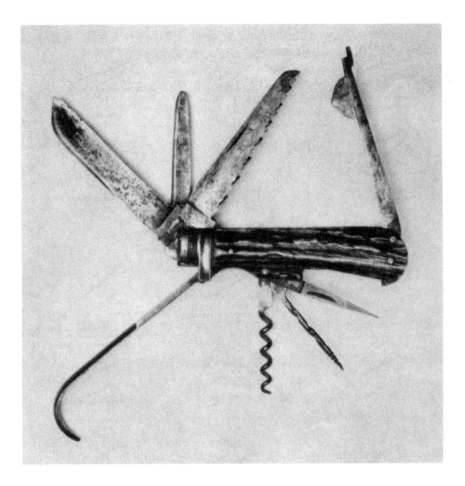

FIGURE
171

Horseman's or farrier's knife of about 1860 with master blade, pen blade, saw or rasp, fleam, punch, gimlet, corkscrew, stone hook and screw driver.

D. J. HARRILL COLLECTION

By the time of the American Civil War this period of knife manufacture was in full swing. Mounted men particularly favored knives with stone hooks to help care for their horses' hooves on the march; and corkscrews were always useful to a foraging soldier. One type which was sold widely at the beginning of the war was a combination knife, fork and spoon. One veteran of the war, John Billings of the Massachusetts Artillery, reminisced about this device in his *Hard Tack and Coffee*:

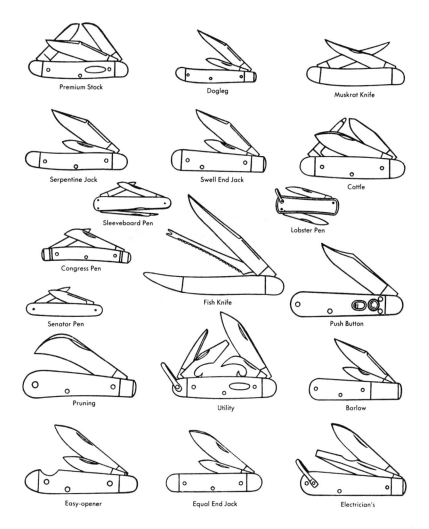

FIGURE
172

Premium Stock

Dogleg

Muskrat Knife

Serpentine Jack

Swell End Jack

Cattle

Sleeveboard Pen

Lobster Pen

Congress Pen

Fish Knife

Senator Pen

Push Button

Pruning

Utility

Barlow

Easy-opener

Equal End Jack

Electrician's

Some of the more popular types of pocketknife made today. FROM The Cutlery Story BY LEWIS D. BEMENT, COURTESY THE ASSOCIATED CUTLERY INDUSTRIES.

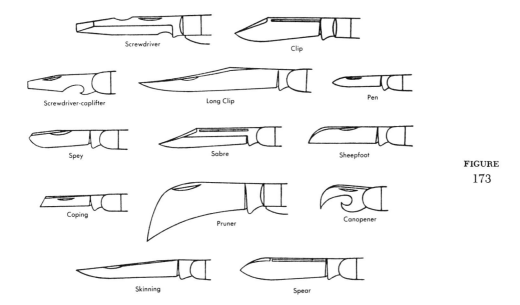

Some standard modern pocketknife blades. FROM The Cutlery Story BY LEWIS D. BEMENT, COURTESY THE ASSOCIATED CUTLERY INDUSTRIES.

FIGURE
173

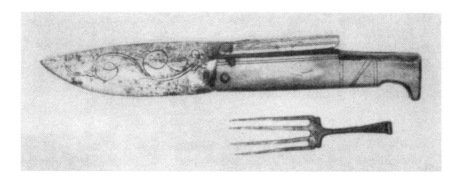

FIGURE
174

Combination folding knife and fork with horn handles probably made in Pennsylvania during the 18th century. JOSEPH AIKEN COLLECTION

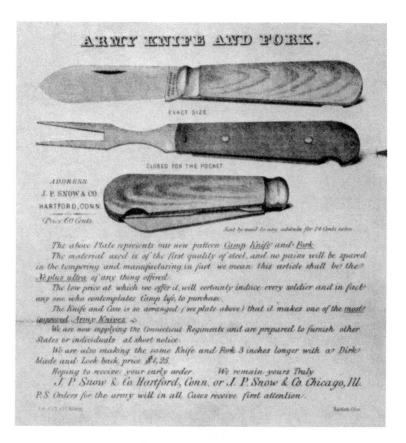

Broadside advertisement for a combination folding knife and fork, 1861.

NATIONAL ARCHIVES

One of the first products of [these inventors'] genius which I recall was a combination *knife-fork-and-spoon* arrangement, which was peddled through the state camping-grounds in great numbers and variety. Of course every man must have one. So much convenience in so small a compass must be taken advantage of. It was a sort of soldier's trinity, which they all thought they understood and appreciated. But I doubt whether this invention, on the average, ever got beyond the first camp in active service.

Three major types of these Civil War knife-fork-spoon combinations are recognized by collectors today, and a few have actually been recovered from battlefield sites.

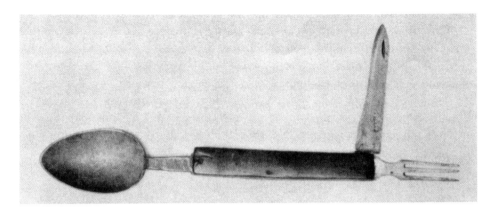

FIGURE
176

Combination knife-fork-and-spoon of the Civil War. This tool could be divided so that the knife was held in one hand and the spoon and fork combined in the other.

FRANCIS A. LORD COLLECTION

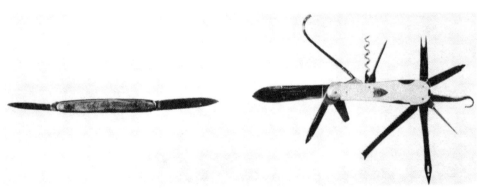

FIGURE
177

Two pocketknives presented to President Grant. The two-bladed knife was made by M. Price of San Francisco. It has a gold handle and was given to Grant by the miners of Warren's Digging in 1873. The larger knife was made by Joseph Rodgers of Sheffield and given to the President in 1877. It has pearl handles and gilt mounts.

U. S. NATIONAL MUSEUM

In more modern times, the soldier or sailor has found the diversified pocketknife of real assistance. During World War II survival knives particularly were issued with a great number of accessory blades. O.S.S. personnel had special knives with wire cutters, saws and can openers; and many seamen had combination knives and marlin spikes.

This has been the general history of pocketknives in America. Times have changed and with them their special requirements. A man no longer needs a knife to trim his pen or sharpen his pencil, but there are still hundreds of uses for a convenient small knife even for the big city office worker. The large pocketknives now are carried primarily by Boy Scouts, farmers or outdoor men. But whatever their occupation or condition, it is a safe estimate that well over ninety percent of all American men own at least one form or another today. Thus, though some 1900 years or more have passed since its invention, it is still the most universal personal knife.

CHAPTER VIII

THE MANUFACTURE AND SHARPENING OF KNIVES

THE man whose life depends on his weapons always holds the man who makes them in high regard. This has been true for all time. The ancients deified the skill of the smith and made offerings to Hephaestus, Vulcan or Thor. Later the armorer was frequently established at court, an intimate of kings and emperors, and a respected personage in his own right. In colonial America the smith was no less important. His function was recognized as essential to the community, and often he was elected to public office.

During the eighteenth and early nineteenth centuries the knives forged in America were made by a process already centuries old. Steel was normally purchased in bars. The smith would take one of these bars and heat it in the forge until it was red hot. Then he would place it on the anvil and hammer it out until it was almost the proper thickness for the blade and had acquired the general shape he wanted. Sometimes he did this job alone. At other times he might have an assistant called a hammerman or

143

striker. In that case the smith would hold the bar with pincers in his left hand and tap it lightly with a small hammer to show the striker where to hit it with his heavier hammer. This forging was a slow process, and the bar would have to be returned to the fire several times for reheating. Sometimes the tang would be forged from the same piece of steel. At other times a piece of iron would be welded to the steel blade. Next came a finer shaping on the anvil, called "smithing." Then the name or mark was stamped in, and the blade was hardened and tempered.

Hardening and tempering a blade are processes which depend solely on temperature and time. The early smiths relied entirely on their eye in judging the color of the metal which indicated the proper heat and their sense of timing in knowing how long to hold it in the various stages.

First the blade was heated until it was cherry red (1450–2000 degrees Fahrenheit, depending on the type of steel). Then it was cooled rapidly by plunging it into water, oil or salts. This left the blade light gray in color and very hard and brittle. To add resiliency and to bring the metal to a suitable hardness for holding an edge, the blade was again heated, this time at a lower temperature. The smith watched as the steel changed color in the forge, first straw color, then brown, purple, dark blue and finally light blue. When it reached the proper color, he withdrew it and cooled it slowly. Generally speaking, the longer the blade was left in the fire, the greater the amount of flexibility the steel would acquire. Thus a blade requiring great hardness, such as a straight razor blade, would be withdrawn when it reached the straw color. A pocketknife blade would be allowed to reach a purple color; while most sheath knives which required a hard yet flexible blade would be drawn at the light blue stage.

There are many stories about secret processes, magic incantations and the use of special water, oil or other liquid for cooling the blades. If any of these were effective, it was solely because they helped assure either the proper temperature or time. Water from certain springs, milk, oil or other liquids from specific sources stored under prescribed conditions might well produce well-tempered blades because of the accident of their temperature. Incantations repeated during the processes might also help because they would require a certain length of time to recite. For this reason a modern artilleryman recites doggerel in timing the guns of a salute.

When a blade had been forged and tempered, it was passed on to a grinder, who gave it its finished form. The grinder sat on a saddle or horsing

FIGURE

178

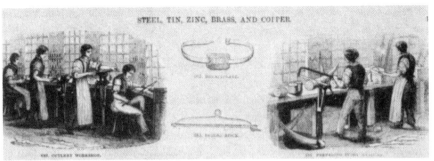

Tools and techniques of knife manufacture in Sheffield. FROM C. TOMLINSON,
Illustrations of Useful Arts and Manufactures, *1859.*

BELLA C. LANDAUER COLLECTION, NEW-YORK HISTORICAL SOCIETY

above a water-driven wheel of natural sandstone. He fastened the blade to
a wooden holder or "flat stick" to protect his hands from the heat caused by
the grinding and began to work. Wheels of many different sizes were used
according to the requirements of the knife. The smaller blades and those
requiring a deep, hollow grind needed smaller wheels; the larger and
flatter blades needed wheels of greater diameter.

Grinding was an important job, demanding great skill. It was also un-
pleasant and dangerous. Much of a knife's efficiency and most of its appearance depended upon the quality of its grinding. The edge depended solely
on the grinder. Balance could be changed, and poor shapes could be improved or good ones ruined by the man at the wheel. Because of this,
grinders took particular pride in their work. At the same time the dust
from the sandstone caused most of the workers to develop "grinders' con-
sumption," a form of silicosis, after only a few years of work. Bursting stones

with fatal or crippling results were also a hazard of the profession until emery wheels replaced the natural sandstone.

After grinding, the blades were polished. Usually this was done on wooden wheels faced with leather or with an alloy of lead and tin or at times with a mixture of tallow and emery. Final polishing was done on a buff dressed with crocus of iron or very fine emery.

When the blade had been polished, it was fitted with its handle. The guard was slipped over the tang, followed by the grips and finally the pommel; and all were riveted in place. Wood or tusks of elephant or walrus ivory for grips were first cut with a small frame saw and then with a small circular saw. Stag horn or antler was softened by boiling and then shaped, while cow and buffalo horn were heated and pressed into iron molds. Pearl and tortoise shell were sawed much the same as ivory and bone, and then all were polished.

These were the steps in the manufacture of a sheath or carving knife, the easiest form of knife to make. A pocketknife was much more complicated, the simplest penknife passing through a workman's hands at least a hundred times. Blades were forged, ground and polished in the manner described. Then springs had to be forged and tempered. The linings were cut from sheet stock, bolsters were cast, and blades, springs, lining and bolsters were drilled with the proper holes and pinned together to see that the parts would fit and work well, open smoothly, fold into the handle at the proper angle to lie flat and at the same time have enough height to leave the nail nick readily accessible. This required expert work and fine tooling. When the parts were so assembled, they were riveted with bits of wire on a small anvil. Then the coverings were cut out and polished twice on the buffs, first with trent sand and then with rotten stone and oil and fastened in place. If there was an escutcheon plate, more steps were added, and every additional blade added to the complexity of the operation.

Until the second quarter of the nineteenth century almost all knives used in America were made in Sheffield, England. Then the American industry began, and with it came changes in the age-old practices. The first American cutlery manufacturer of any size is believed to have been Henry Harrington, who made butcher knives near Worcester, Massachusetts, in 1819. Harrington's work, however, apparently had only local distribution. Then came the Ames brothers, Nathan Peabody and James T. These two

Yankee entrepreneurs set up shop at Chicopee Falls, Massachusetts, in 1829 and began to offer products for general sale in 1830. Their interests were diversified, and perhaps they cannot be labeled categorically either as blacksmiths or cutlers. They were general manufacturers, making almost everything from mill machinery to machine knives and edged tools to table knives and swords. Cutlery was never a major part of their business, but they did produce fine knives and helped open the American market to locally made products.

It remained for John Russell really to found the American cutlery industry. A native of Deerfield, Massachusetts, who had been a jeweler, silversmith and cotton speculator, Russell was attracted to the cutlery business by reading about the Sheffield shops in a book. In 1832 he formed a partnership with his brother Francis and started in business by manufacturing chisels in a shop on the Green River near Deerfield. Meeting with considerable success, he turned to knives, but a disastrous fire and then a spring flood completely destroyed his plants. At this stage a Greenfield banker named Henry Clapp came to his assistance, and in 1836 a partnership was formed with Clapp and the Russell brothers called the John Russell Manufacturing Company.

FIGURE
179

The John Russell Manufacturing Company, about 1870.

The competition from English cutlers was severe, but Russell found ways to overcome it. Americans were prejudiced in favor of Sheffield blades, and English firms began to cut prices in an effort to force him out of business. Russell had to manufacture a fine product, and he had to cut costs. To insure the quality of his knives he imported workers from Sheffield; and to cut costs he developed labor-saving machinery, thereby revolutionizing the cutlers' trade. From the beginning he had used a small steam engine to drive his grinding wheels, but his major innovation was the use of a water-driven trip hammer for forging blades, which vastly speeded production. This was the first time that power had been used for such forging any place in the world. Finally, Russell also developed improved polishing jacks and set up a true assembly-line production.

Under Russell's inspired directorship, the company prospered fabulously. For over twenty-five years the annual value of the products more than doubled each year as the company manufactured table knives, butcher and carving knives, cooks' knives, pocketknives, knife blanks for silver platers and finally hunting knives. The knives were sold all over the country and became so famous in the West that their "Green River" trademark became a symbol of quality or excellence in any line of endeavor.

The John Russell Company became one of America's largest cutlery companies, and it continues in business today. During its long history it has undergone several reorganizations. In 1868 the plant was moved from Greenfield to Turners Falls, Massachusetts, and there the partnership was enlarged and incorporated for the first time. In 1873 the name was changed to the John Russell Cutlery Company. Finally, in 1935, it merged with the John Harrington Company to become the Russell-Harrington Cutlery Company, and the enterprise was moved to Southbridge, Massachusetts.

After Russell came a host of American cutlers, mostly in Massachusetts, Connecticut and New York. In 1835 the Meriden Cutlery Company was founded at Meriden, Connecticut. It manufactured pocketknives primarily. In 1842 Lamson and Goodnow of Shelburne Falls, Massachusetts, began to make cutlery as well as scythe snaths, and by 1860 they were rated the largest cutlery company in America. In 1845 came the Empire Knife Company of West Winsted, Connecticut. In 1853 the New York Knife Company was organized at Walden by a group of knife makers from Sheffield. Walden also housed the Schrade-Walden Cutlery Company, which is today the oldest operating pocketknife company in the United States. Slightly later, but with early roots, was the firm of Landers, Frary & Clark, another Connecticut company. It grew from a series of smaller firms and was finally incorporated in 1865. These are only a few of the many firms which sprang up at mid-century. Later years saw the industry expand at even greater speed.

As the years passed, mechanization increased. More and larger trip hammers were added. Dies were developed which stamped blades and bolsters in one operation. Grinding and polishing wheels were improved until these functions became almost mechanical. Production was speeded, and the need for the old hand skills dwindled and almost disappeared.

In recent years, however, there has been a reaction against this trend. Skilled knife users have come to realize that the machine-made product can never quite equal a custom-made blade carefully designed for the individual owner. Because of this, the few firms which have recently begun to produce hand-forged blades have found a ready market for their knives. The best known of these small shops is that of W. D. Randall, Jr., in Orlando, Florida, who started business in 1936 and now has orders stacked up six months ahead of possible production. Other modern hand craftsmen include W. F. Moran, Jr., of Lime Kiln, Maryland; H. H. Buck & Son of San Diego, California, and the Rauna Knife Works of Bonner, Montana. All find the demand for their knives steadily increasing.

In these modern shops, the electric furnace and the pyrometer have replaced the old forge and the color judgment for temperature, but the other processes remain the same. The blade is still rough-forged and then smithed on the anvil. It is ground and polished individually as the balance and edges are checked. Handles are shaped and fastened in place, and the entire knife subjected to careful scrutiny and testing before it is allowed to leave the shop. Here the old-time skilled worker reigns supreme once more.

Whether a knife is forged by hand or made on an assembly line, it needs constant care if it is to remain an efficient tool or weapon. It must be cleaned after using and when laid aside for any period of time it must be protected from rust. Most important, however, is the maintenance of a sharp edge, and this requires constant attention. Every edge is composed of microscopic teeth, and these must constantly be reset and realigned if the edge is to have its maximum keenness. This is usually done on a steel

FIGURE
180

W. F. Moran, Jr., of Lime Kiln, Maryland, still uses an open forge and tempers by eye while making fine modern knives. Here the steel bar or skelp is heated.

FIGURE
181

When the steel is red-hot, the forging is begun on the anvil.

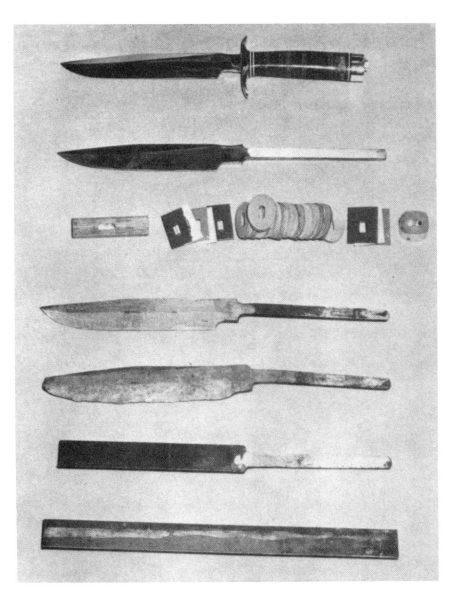

FIGURE
182

Steps in the manufacture of a Randall fighting knife. From bottom to top: the steel bar cut to the proper length; the tang cut to size; the blade forged and smithed; the blade after grinding; the brass bar, leather washers and Duralumin butt cap ready to be assembled and shaped; the polished blade; the finished knife.

William Platts, shop manag
applies the blade of a Rand
knife to the grinder. A pile
blades ready for grinding
at his right.

FIGURE
183

FIGURE
184

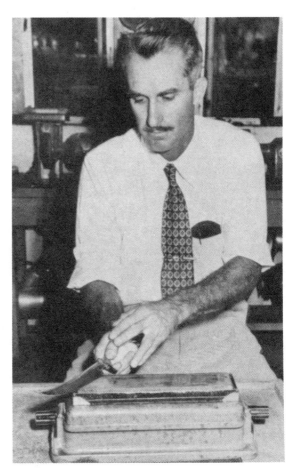

W. D. Randall, Jr., himself applying
the "finish" hone to one of his hunting knives in his Orlando, Florida, shop.

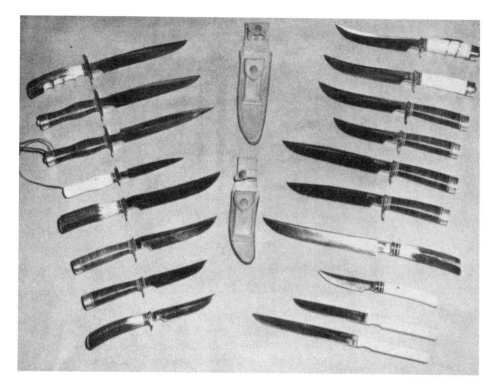

FIGURE
185

Some of the standard models of Randall-made knives produced today. Fighting knives have full cross guards; hunting knives, only one quillon; and carving or fish knives, none at all.

rod. Also from time to time the knife must be resharpened and a new set of these tiny teeth formed. This requires an oilstone, whetstone or other abrasive surface.

Today we have a great variety of sharpening and setting instruments, but this has not always been the case. The soldier or the hunter away from civilization selected natural stones, or, during wartime, even paving blocks in the street. Natural sandstone was preferred, and small pieces have been quarried and kept for that purpose for centuries. Some knife sheaths were made with little pockets for such stones, and the buffalo hunters of the American West usually carried both whetstone and steel with them in

FIGURE
186

*In 1608 Thomas Trevelyan painted this picture of an Eng-
lishman sharpening his butcher knife on a stone as he
prepares to slaughter a pig. The technique has not changed.*
FOLGER SHAKESPEARE LIBRARY

special scabbards. For setting an edge, those who didn't have special steels
often used the steel from their tinder box. It was not well designed for the
purpose, but it could be used, and so it was for centuries. Finally, also,
many a mountaineer and soldier honed his knife to its keenest point on the
thick leather of his boots. However it was done, the result was the same.
The valued knife remained an efficient dependable servant.

APPENDIX

A LIST OF AMERICAN MAKERS, MARKS AND DEALERS

In compiling the present brief guide for knife collectors it was felt that one of its most useful features might be a list of the names and marks that could reasonably be expected to appear on the blades of American sheath and pocket knives. A complete list of such names and marks would be the work of a lifetime. The present list makes no pretense of being complete, but it does represent the gleanings of many years of study by the author and by Benjamin Palmer and William A. Albaugh, III, who generously made their research notes available for this first printed compilation. No name has been included in this list unless there is evidence to indicate that its owner was concerned with the manufacture or sale of sheath or pocket knives and was not merely a producer of razors, scissors, swords, edged tools, table or industrial cutlery.

AMERICAN CUTLERY COMPANY
   Address unknown. Made models 1917 and 1917CT bolos and 1917 and 1918 trench knives.

AMES, JAMES T.
AMES MANUFACTURING COMPANY
AMES, NATHAN P.
AMES, NATHAN P., JR.
   Massachusetts. Nathan P. Ames finished his apprenticeship as a bladesmith in 1791 and set up shop in Chelmsford, Mass. His sons, Nathan P., Jr., and James T. Ames learned the trade from their father, and in 1829 the shop was moved to Chicopee Falls, Mass. In 1834 the Ames Manufacturing Company was formed with a capital of $30,000. Plants were subsequently established both in Cabotville and Springfield, Mass., as the Company became more and more diversified. Cutlery products included table knives, machine knives, swords, the famous 1849 rifleman's knife and the Dahlgren bowie bayonet among other items.

BABBITT, L. W.
   Cleveland, Ohio. Made hunting knives 1832–1838.

BACON, WILLIAM
   New York City. Cutler and gunsmith before and after 1843.

BAKER, JOHN
   Address unknown. Made bowie knives for the state of Georgia, delivering at least 300 in April and May 1862.

157

BARTLETT EDGE TOOL COMPANY
Address unknown. Made models 1917 and 1917CT bolos.

BAY STATE HARDWARE COMPANY
Northampton, Mass. Founded in 1863, the company first began to make cutlery in 1868. It went bankrupt in 1871 and was reorganized as the Northampton Cutlery Company.

BELL & DAVIS
Atlanta, Ga. The name, address and date July 6, 1861, are inscribed on a bowie knife with a knuckle-bow.

BERKSHIRE CUTLERY COMPANY
Address unknown. The name appears on a folding dirk-knife of the 1870's.

BERRY, WILL
Address unknown. Made bowie knives for the state of Georgia in 1862.

B. G. I. CO.
Mark of the Bridgeport Gun Implement Company, q.v.

BLACK, JAMES
Washington, Arkansas. In later life Black, a noted cutler and silversmith, claimed to have made the "original" bowie knife as an improvement on a model submitted by Bowie himself.

BLITTERSDORF, C. J.
143 N. 4th Street, Philadelphia. Cutler before and after 1849.

BOKER, H., & COMPANY
New York City. Modern cutler making "Tree Brand" knives.

BOWN & SON

BOWN & TETLEY
136-138 Wood Street, Pittsburgh. James Bown founded the firm of Bown & Tetley in 1848 and became sole proprietor in 1862. In 1871 his son, William, joined him in business as James Bown & Son. See figures 62 and 75.

BOYLE & GAMBLE

BOYLE, GAMBLE & MACFEE
Richmond, Va. Made swords and bayonets, including a bowie bayonet, for the Confederacy.

BRIDDELL, CHARLES D., INC.
Crisfield, Maryland. Modern cutler.

BRIDGEPORT GUN IMPLEMENT COMPANY
Bridgeport, Conn. Organized about the turn of the twentieth century, the firm used its initials as its mark on knives—"B. G. I. CO." See figure 76.

BROOKS ARMS & TOOL COMPANY
Portland, Maine. Made belt knives, 1890–1893.

BUCK, H. H., & SON
San Diego, California. Modern makers of hand-forged knives.

BUELL, ABEL
Main Street, Hartford, Conn. In 1799 he advertised "Silver plated, gilt, steel, brass and iron hilted swords and dirks, pikes, and military flags."

BURGER & BROS.

Richmond, Va. Advertised in 1861 for cutlery grinders and a blacksmith to work on swords, bayonets and bowie knives. The factory was located at the Petersburg Railroad bridge. Burger had been in the saw-making business with Edwin Boyle of Boyle, Gamble and MacFee prior to the war.

CAMERON & WINN

Address unknown. Made bowie knives for the state of Georgia. At least 458 were delivered from April until June, 1862.

CAMILLUS CUTLERY COMPANY

Camillus, N. Y. Made many of the combat knives during World War II.

CASE, W. R.

CASE, W. R., & SONS COMPANY

Bradford, Pa. Cutlers still in business making "Case Knives" and "Case XX" brand. During World War II, they manufactured the M3 Army trench knife and the experimental V-42 commando-type knife.

CATTARAUGUS CUTLERY COMPANY

Little Valley, N. Y. Modern makers of "Cattaraugus" knives.

CHATILLON, JOHN, & SONS COMPANY

New York City. Modern makers of "Foster" knives. During World War II, they produced medical corpsman's knives for the Marine Corps.

CHEVALIER, JOHN D.

New York City. John D. Chevalier appears in the New York City directories from 1835 until 1869 with many different street addresses. Most of his entries refer to him as a maker of dental and surgical instruments, chairs, false teeth, etc. In 1852/53 and again in 1854/55 he is listed as a cutler. In 1861/62 the firm became John D. Chevalier and Sons. Chevalier bowie knives dated from the 1852–55 period have been identified, and the workmanship is excellent. Some bear his name and the address (which at that time was 360 Broadway); others are marked "CHEVALIER'S CALIFORNIA KNIFE."

CHICAGO GUN & CUTLERY COMPANY

Chicago. Made hunting knives, 1887–1895.

CLARK, DANIEL

Middle Ward, Philadelphia. Cutlery dealer before and after 1850.

CLARKSON & CO.

106 Main Street, Richmond, Va. Advertised "Virginia-made Bowie knives at reduced prices" in December 1861.

CLARKSON, ANDERSON & CO.

106 Main Street, Richmond, Va. Advertised pistols and bowie knives for sale in June 1861.

CLEMENT COMPANY, THE

CLEMENT CUTLERY COMPANY

CLEMENT, W. T.

Northampton, Mass. W. T. Clement was at one time an employee of Lamson & Goodnow. Later he set up shop for himself and in 1857 joined in partnership to purchase the bankrupt Bay State Tool Company which he reorganized in 1866 as the Clement-Hawks Manufacturing Company. This company also failed, and in 1882 he organized the Clement Cutlery Company. Today it is known as The Clement Company and manufactures "Delvin" knives.

CLYDE CUTLERY COMPANY

Clyde, Ohio. Modern makers of "Clyde" knives.

COLLINS & COMPANY

Collinsville, Connecticut. Established in 1826 by Samuel W. Collins, Daniel C. Collins and William Wells, Collins & Company have been primarily manufacturers of axes, plows and machetes. During the Civil War, however, they did produce sword blades. About the same time they appear to have begun the manufacture of a limited number of knives. Despite the fact that the factory was at Collinsville, the address "Hartford" is always used on genuine Collins products. See figure 102.

COLONIAL CUTLERY COMPANY

Providence, R. I. Modern makers of "Colonial" knives.

CORSA DENTON, BURDEKAN & CO.

Address unknown. The name appears on post-Civil War knives which seem to be of American manufacture.

CROOKS, JONATHAN

Address unknown. The name appears on knives of the Civil War era which seem to be American. Sometimes there is also the trade mark "Tip" alongside a drawing of a top.

"DELVIN"

Trade mark of The Clement Company, q.v.

DISSTON, HENRY, & SONS

Philadelphia. Designed the model 1917 trench knife.

DOBBY WYCHETT

Address unknown. The name appears on a late nineteenth-century knife that seems to be American made.

DODGE, SIMON F.

Winchester, Va. Made bowie knives during the Civil War.

EKCO PRODUCTS COMPANY

Chicago. Modern makers of "Flint" and "Geneva Forge" knives.

"EMPIRE"

Trade mark of The Voos Company, q.v.

EMPIRE KNIFE COMPANY

West Winsted, Conn. Established in 1845.

ENGLISH, J.

Philadelphia. The name appears on large bowie knives marked "Sheffield Works/2/, Philadephia." See figure 43.

ETOWAH IRON WORKS

Georgia. Made bowie knives for the Atlanta Grays in 1861, which were described as "handsomely mounted, of excellent workmanship and most beautiful finish."

"EVERLASTINGLY SHARP"
Trade mark of the Schrade-Walden Cutlery Company, q.v.

FINCK, JULIUS
San Francisco. Partner of Frederick A. Will. See Will & Finck.

FITZPATRICK, CAPT. REES
Natchez, Miss. On June 8, 1861 an article appeared in the Richmond *Examiner* describing a knife made by Fitzpatrick for Dr. L. P. Blackburn who planned to show it to the armorers of Louisville as a pattern for those they were to make for defense of the state. Fitzpatrick is also represented in this article as having been the first to adapt the bowie for use as a bayonet and to have made the original knife of Col. James Bowie himself.

"FLINT"
Trade mark of the Ekco Products Company, q.v.

FORD, J. J.
Address unknown. Made bowie knives for the state of Georgia, delivering 136 in June, 1862.

"FOSTER"
Trade mark of John Chatillon & Sons Company, q.v.

FOSTER BROTHERS
Address unknown. The name appears on an apparently American make knife of the 1860–1880 period with the legend "BUFFALO CLEAVER" and a trade mark of a diamond pierced by an arrow.

"GENEVA FORGE"
Trade mark of the Ekco Products Company, q.v.

G. GELSTON MANUFACTURING COMPANY
Address unknown. The name appears on a late nineteenth century knife that is apparently American made.

GILLELAND, H.
Address unknown. Made bowie knives for the state of Georgia, delivering 40 during May, 1862.

GITTER & MOSS
Beal Street, Memphis, Tenn. Advertised December 12, 1861, that they were fitted up to produce swords, knives, and all other kinds of Army cutlery.

GOODELL COMPANY, THE
Antrim, N. H. Modern makers of "Goodell" knives.

GOSLING, RICHARD
Philadelphia. Made knives and belt axes, 1714–1717.

GRAVELEY & WREAKS
New York. The name appears on an early bowie knife made by W. S. Butcher of Sheffield. New York City directories failed to reveal any such firm, but there were Wreakses in the importing business in 1835–1840. See figure 51.

GRAY, JOHN D.
Address unknown. Made bowie knives for the state of Georgia, delivering 600 in May and August, 1862.

GREAVES, W., & SONS

Address unknown. The name appears on a knife of the Civil War era that seems to be of American manufacture.

GREEN RIVER

GREEN RIVER WORKS

Marks of the John Russell Manufacturing Company and the John Russell Cutlery Company, q.v. Also sometimes pirated by English cutlers. See figures 94 and 95.

HAIL, F. M.

Address unknown. Made bowie knives for the state of Georgia, delivering 49 in June 1862.

HALL, JAMES M.

Address unknown. Made bowie knives for the state of Georgia, delivering 15 in April, 1862.

"HAMMER BRAND"

Trade mark of the Imperial Knife Company, q.v.

HARRINGTON, HENRY

Worcester, Mass. He made butcher knives near Worcester in 1819.

HASSAM

HASSAM BROTHERS

Boston, Mass. Both names appear on bowie knives of the pre-Civil War and Civil War eras. See figure 63.

HATCH CUTLERY COMPANY

South Milwaukee, Wis. Organized in the late nineteenth century, they manufactured a wide variety of knives.

HAYNES, O. S.

Address unknown. Made bowie knives for the state of Georgia, delivering 49 on April 12, 1862.

HENDRICKS, JOHN

Philadelphia. Made belt knives and trade tomahawks, 1783–1790.

HICKS, ANDREW G.

Cleveland, Ohio. A cutler and tool maker who seems to have been active from the late 1830's through at least 1859 when the Cleveland *Leader* described him as an "old traveler." He made fine rifleman's knives, possibly under contract to the Allegany Arsenal. See figures 96 and 97.

HUBER

Philadelphia. The name, almost obliterated, appears on large bowie knives also marked "Sheffield Works/2/Philadelphia." The words "Huber Steel" also appear on American-made knives of the late 1830's and early 1840's. See figure 43.

HUGHES, R. J.

Address unknown. Made bowie knives for the state of Georgia, delivering 1,469 during April and May, 1862.

HUNTER, ALFRED

Address unknown. The name appears on well-made knives of the pre-Civil

War era. No address is given, and there is disagreement among students as to whether he was American or English. See figure 41.

HYDE MANUFACTURING COMPANY

Southbridge, Mass. Modern makers of "Hyde" knives.

IMPERIAL KNIFE COMPANY

Providence, R. I. Modern makers of "Hammer Brand" and "Jackmaster Brand" knives.

"JACKMASTER BRAND"

Trade mark of the Imperial Knife Company, q.v.

JOHN HARRINGTON COMPANY

Southbridge, Mass. The John Harrington Company was founded sometime before 1850 and specialized in table cutlery. In 1935 it merged with the John Russell Manufacturing Company, q.v.

JOHN RUSSELL CUTLERY COMPANY

JOHN RUSSELL MANUFACTURING COMPANY

Greenfield and Turners Falls, Mass. In 1832 John Russell, a native of Deerfield, Mass., and a jeweler and silversmith, formed a partnership with his brother, Francis, to manufacture chisels in a shop on the Green River near Deerfield. Meeting with considerable success, they turned to knives, but their plant was destroyed by a fire and a flood. In 1836 with Henry Clapp, a Greenfield banker, they founded the John Russell Manufacturing Company with a factory still on the Green River but nearer Greenfield. In it, Russell pioneered in applying power-driven machines to the production of cutlery and so revolutionized the business. In 1868, the plant was moved from Greenfield to Turners Falls, and in 1873 the name was changed to the John Russell Cutlery Company. Finally, in 1935 it merged with the John Harrington Company to become the Russell-Harrington Cutlery Company.

The Russell Company made all manner of kitchen, butcher, table and pocket knives, and in later years made some hunting knives. All were of the highest quality. The Russell Barlow knives were a byword among all boys half a century ago. And the "Green River" trade mark of the other knives became a symbol of quality in the early West. The early fixed-bladed knives were usually stamped "J. RUSSELL & CO./GREEN RIVER WORKS" in two lines. Later a diamond-shaped stamp was placed below it. Sometime before 1890 the Company changed from stamped to etched marks, and finally, the commemorative date, 1834, was added to some. Pocket knives, especially the Barlows, were usually stamped on the bolster with a special trade mark consisting of a capital "R" pierced by an arrow. See figures 78, 92, 93, 154, 156, 168, 179.

JONES, BENJAMIN

Tredyffrine, Pa. He made belt knives of the "bowie" type 1775–1781.

"KA-BAR"

Trade mark of the Union Cutlery Company, q.v.

KESMODEL, FRANK

San Francisco. Partner of Frederick Will in 1862. See Will & Finck.

KINFOLKS, INC.

Little Valley, N. Y. Modern makers of "Kinfolks" knives. During World War II, they made M3 trench knives.

KNIGHT'S BLACKSMITH SHOP

Amelia, Virginia. Made bowie knives for the Confederacy.

KRAFT, PETER W.

184 Main Street, Columbia, S. C. Advertised bowie knives for sale in January 1861.

"KUTMASTER"

Trade mark of the Utica Cutlery Company, q.v.

LAMSON & GOODNOW MANUFACTURING COMPANY

Shelburne Falls, Mass. In 1842 Ebnezer and Nathanial Lamson began to manufacture cutlery in addition to their production of scythe snathes. The business prospered, and in 1844, Abel F. and Ebnezer Goodnow joined them to form the Lamson & Goodnow Manufacturing Company. By 1860 they were rated the largest cutlery company in America. The gun-making firm of Lamson, Goodnow and Yale was somewhat interlocking in directorate, but was an entirely separate company at Windsor, Vermont. See figures 77 and 155.

LAN & SHERMAN

Cary Street above 9th, Richmond, Va. Advertised that they made bowie knives from the finest file steel, May 1861.

LANDERS, FRARY & CLARK

New Britain, Conn. In 1865, the firm was incorporated with a capital of $250,000, but the manufacture of cutlery apparently was not begun until 1866. The first cutlery products were table knives, but other types were gradually added, and by 1903 the Company was rated the largest producer of cutlery in the world. See figures 76 and 109.

MARBLE ARMS & MANUFACTURING COMPANY

Gladstone, Michigan. Organized by W. L. Marble in 1898, the firm still makes hunting knives.

MCCONNELL, HUGH

San Francisco. McConnell is reputed to have made butcher and bowie knives as early as 1852, but he is not listed in the San Francisco directory until 1854 when he had a shop at 116 Pacific Street. Thereafter he appears each year as a manufacturing cutler and instrument maker—at 233 Jackson Street from 1856 to 1858; at 191 Jackson in 1859 and 1860, and finally at 605 Jackson to 1861 and 1862. In 1863 he was succeeded at that address by Frederick A. Will. Of McConnell it has been said that he made bowie knives "of excellent temper and mounted with silver or even gold, in such manner that a knife sold for $100 or more."

MCELROY, W. J., & CO.

Macon, Ga. A tin shop operator before the War, he turned to making munitions at the outbreak of hostilities. According to DeBow's *Review*, he manufactured 20 infantry swords, bowie knives, naval cutlasses, sergeant's swords, sword belts, and straps for same a week, 50 brass cavalry spurs a week and an unknown number of bayonets, tin canteens and pikes. All of his products that have been studied were of the highest quality. See figure 70.

MCKINSTRY, ALEXANDER

Address unknown. Alabama purchased 1,000 bowie knives for the use of the 48th Regiment Alabama Militia from him in 1861.

MERIDEN CUTLERY COMPANY

Meriden, Conn. Incorporated in 1855 by Julius Pratt and David Ropes. See Ropes, David.

MOORE, J. W. & L. L.

Address unknown. Made bowie knives for the state of Georgia, delivering 843 in April and May, 1862.

MORAN, W. F., JR.

Lime Kiln, Md. Modern maker of fine custom-made hand-forged bowie knives. See figures 180, 181.

MORRISON, MURDOCH

Rockingham County, N. C. Made bowie knives and pistols on a small scale in 1862.

MURRAY, JOHN P.

46 Broad Street, Columbus, Ga. Advertised as successor to Hoppolt and Murray listing knives, firearms and equipment for sale, July 1862.

NEW YORK KNIFE COMPANY

Walden, N. Y. Established in 1853 by a group of cutlers from Sheffield.

NORTHAMPTON CUTLERY COMPANY

Northampton, Mass. Organized from the Bay State Hardware Company after it had gone bankrupt in 1871, the Northampton Company produced butcher, hunting and carving knives.

ONEIDA COMMUNITY, LTD.

Oneida, N. Y. Made the model 1917 and 1918 trench knives.

ONTARIO KNIFE COMPANY

Franklinville, N. Y. Modern makers of "Tru-Edge" knives.

OPPLEMAN, L.

Lynchburg, Va. The name and address appear on an American bowie knife.

PAL BLADE & TOOL COMPANY

Plattsburg, N. Y. Made the M3 trench knife during World War II.

PEABODY, HIRAM

High Street, Richmond, Va. Cutlery dealer who sold bowie knives before and after 1850–1860.

PETTIBONE, DANIEL

Philadelphia, Pa. Gunsmith, cutler and U. S. inspector of arms, 1808, 1809, who also made pikes in 1812 as well as belt axes and knives.

PLUMB, FAYETTE R.

St. Louis, Mo. Made models 1917 and 1917CT bolos.

PRATT ROPES COMPANY

Meriden, Conn. See Ropes, David.

PRICE, MICHAEL

San Francisco. Price first appears in the San Francisco directories in 1859 at 59 Montgomery Street. In 1861 he moved to 221 Montgomery; in 1862 to 238 Montgomery; in 1863 to 110 Montgomery. Sometime after 1868 he moved to 415 Kearny Street and also opened a factory at 23 Stevenson Street. He died in late 1888 or early 1889, for the directory of that year lists his estate. His mark was often a simple two-line stamp "M.PRICE/S.F." See figure 177.

"Q"

QUEEN CUTLERY COMPANY

Titusville, Pa. Modern makers of "Q" brand knives.

QUIKUT, INC.

Fremont, Ohio. Modern makers of "Quikut" knives.

RANDALL, W. D., JR.

Orlando, Fla. Modern maker of fine hand-forged knives for hunting and fighting, since 1936. See figures 80, 116, 182, 183, 184, and 185.

RAUNA KNIFE WORKS

Bonner, Montana. Modern makers of hand-forged sheath knives.

REINHARDT & BROTHER

REINHARDT, CHARLES C.

REINHARDT, CHARLES C., & COMPANY

REINHARDT, CHARLES, JR.

Baltimore, Md. Charles Reinhardt first appears in the Baltimore directory of 1840/41 as a surgical instrument maker at 24 Lombard Street. In 1842 he moved to 8 Light Street, and in 1845 he organized as Charles C. Reinhardt & Company and moved to 9 Light Street. In 1849 Reinhardt first listed his concern as cutlers as well as surgical and dental instrument makers, but he may well have made knives before that time. In 1856/57 the firm moved to 11 Light Street and then a year later to 7 North Gay Street. In 1865 the firm was reorganized as Reinhardt & Brother (William H. Reinhardt and J. Reinhardt) and Charles C. left the company. The cutlery entry was also dropped in that year. Finally, in 1868, Charles Jr. succeeded to the firm but remained only one year. See figures 40 and 60.

RICHARDS & TAYLOR

RICHARDS, TAYLOR & WILDER

RICHARDS, UPSON & COMPANY

145 Pearl Street, New York City. Military and naval outfitters whose names occasionally appear on dirks. The New York directories list Richards, Upson & Company from 1808–1816. In 1817 it becomes Richard and Taylor, and in 1818 Richards, Taylor & Wilder. See figure 121.

ROBY, C., & COMPANY

West Chelmsford and North Chelmsford, Mass. As cutlery manufacturers, the Roby Company made many swords during the Civil War and also a few knives. Prior to 1863, the firm was located at West Chelmsford. In 1864 and 1865, it was situated in North Chelmsford. See figure 67.

ROPES, DAVID

Saccarapa, Maine, and Meriden, Conn. Ropes established his cutlery shop in 1832. In buying ivory handles for his knives he came in contact with Julius Pratt of Meriden, Conn., an ivory-button maker who also produced excellent knife handles. In 1846 Ropes moved to Meriden and formed a partnership with Pratt as the Pratt Ropes Company. In 1855, the partners incorporated as the Meriden Cutlery Company, q.v.

ROSE

New York City. The name "ROSE/NEW YORK" appears on a bowie knife of the 1845–1855 era. This might have referred to Peter Rose who was listed as a surgical-instrument maker in the New York directory of 1845/46, or Conrad or William H. who were listed in the 1850/51 directory as blacksmiths, or even Joseph, Jr., who listed himself in the latter year as a gunsmith.

RUSSELL-HARRINGTON CUTLERY COMPANY

Southbridge, Mass. Founded in 1935 by a merger of the John Harrington Company and the John Russell Cutlery Company, q.v.

RUSSELL, JOHN

Greenfield, Mass. Founder of the John Russell Manufacturing Company, q.v.

SCHRADE, S.

Bridgeport, Conn. Made M2 paratrooper knives during World War II.

SCHRADE-WALDEN CUTLERY COMPANY

Walden, N. Y. Combination of the old Schrade and Walden knife companies, makers of "Schrade" and "Everlastingly Sharp" knives.

SEARLES

Baton Rouge, La. Searles' name and the Baton Rouge address appear on a brass plate inset in the back of the blades of the knives which Rezin P. Bowie had made to present to friends. See figure 32.

SHEFFIELD WORKS 2

Philadelphia. This appears to have been an American attempt to benefit from the current high regard for cutlery made in Sheffield, England. The name appears on large well-made knives of the 1840's or late 1830's. Usually there are also the names J. ENGLISH and HUBER or possibly MUSER. Three knives so marked have been examined, but in each case the stamping of the last name was so light it had almost been obliterated. See figure 43.

SHELDON, NASH

Eighth Street east of Broadway, Cincinnati, Ohio. Made belt knives 1853–1861.

SMITH, J. W.

Address unknown. Made bowie knives for the state of Georgia, delivering 105 in April and May, 1862.

SMITHWICK, NOAH

San Felipe, Texas. In later years he claimed that Bowie had him copy his famous knife so that he could have a duplicate. This created such a demand that he started a factory selling similar knives for from five to twenty dollars apiece according to finish.

SNOW, J. P., & COMPANY

Hartford, Conn., and Chicago, Ill. Advertised folding dirk knives and combination knife, fork and spoons during the Civil War. See figure 175.

SOMMIS

Providence, R. I. The name appears on a large well-made knife of the 1840–1860 era. See figure 45.

STATON, JOHN L.

Scottsville, Va. Advertised that he could make swords and bowie knives "in the best manner" in July 1861.

SUTHERLAND, SAMUEL

132 Main Street, Richmond, Va. General sporting goods dealer, advertised knives in 1859. During the Civil War he was active as a gunsmith for both the state and the Confederate government.

TAYLOR, G. W.

Address unknown. The name, with the words "cast steel," appears on a knife of the 1860–1875 period that seems to be of American manufacture.

TODD, JOHN

New Orleans, La. He is often reputed to have made a knife for James Bowie in the early 1830's.

TREE BRAND

Trade mark of H. Boker & Company, q.v.

"TRU-EDGE"

Trade mark of the Ontario Knife Company, q.v.

TRYON & BROTHER

TRYON, EDWARD K.

TRYON, GEORGE W.

Philadelphia. The Tryon Company has been a Philadelphia institution since George W. Tryon first established the business at 165 N. Second Street in 1811. Essentially gunsmiths, the Tryons also sold other sporting equipment, including knives which were made for them in England. Usually these knives bore the Tryon name with the words "made in England." Some also bore the trade mark "3/T—Tryon-Tru-Temper." It is not known when this mark was first introduced, but it continued in use until about 1938. The Company changed names and addresses several times: 1829—moved to 134 N. Second Street (now No. 220); 1836 it became George W. Tryon & Co.; 1841, Edward K. Tryon & Co.; 1843 simply Edw. K. Tryon; 1859 back to Edw. K. Tryon & Company with a new store at 625 Market Street; 1863, Tryon & Brother; 1866, Tryon Brothers & Company; 1868, Edw. K. Tryon, Jr. & Company; 1905, Edward K. Tryon Company, Inc. See figure 44.

ULSTER KNIFE COMPANY

New York City. Modern makers of "Ulster" knives.

UNION CAR WORKS

Portsmouth, Va. Manufactured bowie knives and saber bayonets as well as gun carriages, wagons, camp-stools, tent-poles and tent pins for the Confederacy.

UNION CUTLERY COMPANY

Olean, N. Y. Modern makers of "Ka-Bar" knives. During World War II they manufactured knives for both the Marine Corps and the Navy.

UTICA CUTLERY COMPANY

Utica, N. Y. Modern makers of "Kutmaster" knives.

VOOS COMPANY, THE

New Haven, Conn. Modern makers of "Voos" and "Empire" knives.

WADE & BUTCHER

Jersey City, N. J. Modern makers of hunting knives.

WALDEN KNIFE COMPANY

Walden, N. Y. Believed to be a descendant of the New York Knife Company, established in Walden in 1853.

WALKER, WILLIAM

Salt Lake City, Utah. Walker is reputed to have been the first manufacturing cutler west of the Rockies, making knives, razors and scissors at Salt Lake City in 1851.

WEED, N.

Address unknown. Made bowie knives for the state of Georgia, delivering 196 in April 1862.

WELCH, JAMES

St. Charles Street, Richmond, Va., "7 doors above the St. Charles Hotel." General arms dealer, advertised bowie knives and dirks in March 1861.

WESTERN STATE CUTLERY COMPANY

Boulder, Colorado. Modern makers of "Western Cutlery."

WIGFAL, SAMUEL

Philadelphia. Made belt knives 1770–1776.

WILKINSON, H.

Hartford, Conn. The name and address appear on a knife of the 1860–1880 era. It is not known whether this was an independent manufacturer or an outlet for the noted H. Y. Wilkinson cutlery company of England.

WILL, FREDERICK A.

WILL & FINCK

WILLS & FINCK

San Francisco. Frederick Will claimed to have established his cutlery business in California as early as 1852. He first appears in the San Francisco directory of 1861 as a cutler with a residence at 817 Kearny Street but no business address. In 1862 he was listed as a cutler with Frank Kesmodel, dwelling at 904 Powell Street. In 1863 he succeeded to the business of Hugh McConnell at 605 Jackson Street, and in 1864 he formed his partnership with Julius Finck at that address, listing themselves as "cutlers, surgical instrument makers, locksmiths and bell-hangers." (Finck was the locksmith and bell-hanger.) In 1865 the firm moved to 613 Jackson Street. The firm continued in business at various addresses through 1933. It is interesting to note that although the firm name was "Will & Finck," knives are known clearly marked "Wills & Fink/S.F. Cal." See figure 87.

WILLIAM ROGERS MANUFACTURING COMPANY

Hartford, Conn. Manufactured pocket knives and razors, beginning about the middle of the nineteenth century.

ZIMMERMAN, J. C., & CO.

Address unknown. Made bowie knives for the state of Georgia, delivering 209 in April 1862.

INDEX

INDEX